calm™

The Key to Clarity, Connectedness and Presence at Work

Mark Jamieson

Copyright © 2015 Mark Jamieson

Published by The Calm Revolution, Singapore

All rights reserved. No part of this book may be reproduced or transmitted in any form or by any means, electronic or mechanical, including photocopying, recording, faxing, emailing, and posting online or by any information storage and retrieval system, without written permission from the Publisher. All trademarks referred to herein are the property of their respective owners.

For more information contact info@thecalmrevolution.com

Cover and Internal Design by Sheamus Burns

Illustrations by Tim Hamons

ISBN: 978-981-09-2853-7

To my family, friends, and colleagues: you have borne the brunt of my lifelong investigation of myself and of the people who are close to me. Life to me has always has been a great experiment, finding out what works and what doesn't, in all areas of our humanity, and you have been very willing participants.

Calm: The Key to Clarity, Connectedness, and Presence at Work

"We can never obtain peace in the outer world until we make peace with ourselves."

— Dalai Lama XIV

CONTENTS

FOREWORD by Ho Kwon Ping
   From Mindless Busyness to Mindful Business......................iii

INTRODUCTION
   I'm Calm, Now What?..1

PART I: THE CALM APPROACH 15

   1. For Goodness Sake, CALM DOWN! 17
   2. Find the Root CAUSE 35
   3. Be AWARE of How You Think 51
   4. Let It Go 63
   5. Getting in the MOOD 73

PART II: APPLICATIONS 91

   6. Less Stress, More Success 93
   7. Too Busy to Think Straight 105
   8. From There to Here 111
   9. Clarity is the Key 119
   10. Meetings Transformed 127
   11. Putting Off Procrastination 135

PART III: WRAP UP 143

   12. Pollyanna Was Right 145

EPILOGUE 149
ACKNOWLEDGMENTS 151
ABOUT THE AUTHOR 155

FOREWORD
From mindless busyness
to mindful business

Ho Kwon Ping

Founder and Executive Chairman, Banyan Tree Holdings
Chairman of the Board of Trustees, Singapore Management University

Sometimes – and all too rarely now, -- I consciously pause in the midst of daily busy-ness or business, and try to silently take stock of my life around me. I try to become acutely aware of my immediate surroundings and all its details, and as I become more detached, like a person watching myself from above, I grow increasingly aware of my life. In this state of reflective detachment -- usually when I look out over clouds during a long flight – I sometimes achieve a sense of not so much meditative peace, but more a mindful awareness.

This state of detached yet extremely clear awareness of oneself is the essence of mindfulness. It is paradoxically, to be so aware of oneself that one becomes increasingly detached, and one's ego, or self, is stripped away like the layers of an so that one can perceive the world without these distorting layers of the self.

This practice is quite common for many who've grown up in an Asian culture where elements of detachment and self-reflection are core to the practice of Buddhism and Hinduism. How though, might this be relevant to the practice of leadership and management? This question came to mind when, in the course of my work with business education, I wondered whether the paradigms of leadership which came from Western cultural traditions could be augmented and indeed enriched, by Asian cultural traditions.

I think the practice of mindfulness is that contribution. If I had to express it as a *ko-an*, the insightful riddles of Zen Buddhism, it might well be: *Look for your enemy in the mirror.*

Mindfulness provides us the critical insight that it is our own self – our ego --which is the greatest obstacle to making the right decision. And therefore, by being paradoxically always keenly aware of our own self and our total surroundings as we engage the world, we are able to reach that state of calm from which the right decision becomes clear. We do not make a decision; the decision becomes apparent as we de-clutter our minds through mindfulness. When you take yourself out of the picture, the way forward presents itself with clarity and forcefulness.

Business education – and the teaching of leadership with its emphasis on courage, decisiveness and other attributes of the macho Alpha-male – has to put it mildly, failed. The notion of the action-oriented Hero-CEO has in many ways been the result of leadership training. We need new paradigms of leadership and management, whose basis is rooted in mindfulness. This understanding of mindfulness has to be logical, practical and appropriate to the business environment. This book attempts to answer that call.

Singapore Management University is uniquely placed at the intersection of eastern philosophical tradition and western management thinking, which is why I am especially pleased that "calm" was developed here in Singapore. Both traditions have their place.

The western perspective is goal-orientated, logical, and values speed of execution. Its stories are of forcefulness and determination. Leaders are expected to define strategy, set key performance indicators and monitor their progress in minute detail. This model assumes predictability, or more correctly, tries to impose predictability on a resistant world.

The eastern perspective is more purpose-orientated, organic and opportunistic. Its stories are of wisdom and inclusiveness. Its view of reality is of an all-encompassing, indefinable, formless whole, of which we a privy to only a glimpse. Our thoughts are a limited expression of an underlying wisdom. It is more at ease with uncertainty, and tries to accommodate itself to a changing world.

Both perspectives have their place and are needed. They are in fact two aspects of the same underlying reality. However, in the business world the balance has been tipped for some time in favor of the systematic structured approach.

CALM provides a paradigm of mindfulness that explains the true relationship between our mind, our thinking and our awareness, and follows it up with practical examples of how to use it in our working lives. It is perhaps this paradigm that integrates mindfulness into our working lives and incorporates both western and eastern thinking, and acknowledges all of the things that happen in our working life and our home life. We don't leave ourselves behind when we arrive at work, nor should we.

Finding this inner peace and poise may seem the work of a lifetime, but the answer turns out to be simpler than we thought, and in line with what we suspected: We are making things too complicated for ourselves.

How do we know we have got there? We are calm, centred, and insightful.

May you too find the truth of who you really are, so you can live a rich, full and authentic life.

Ho Kwon Ping

About Ho Kwon Ping

The founder of the Banyan Tree Group, Mr Ho Kwon Ping is responsible for its overall management and operations. Mr Ho is also Chairman of Laguna Resorts & Hotels Public Company Limited, Thai Wah Food Products Public Company Limited, the Board of Trustees of Singapore Management University and the Advisory Committee of the School of Hotel and Tourism Management at the Hong Kong

Polytechnic University. He is a non-executive Director of Diageo Plc. He is a member of the International Council and East Asia Council of INSEAD as well as the Global Advisory Board of Moelis & Company, and a Governor of the London Business School.

He previously served as a Chairman of MediaCorp Pte. Ltd.

INTRODUCTION

I'm Calm, Now What?

> *Before enlightenment, chop wood, carry water.*
> *After enlightenment, chop wood, carry water.*
>
> – Zen Proverb

Imagine you're flying Business Class from Singapore to Sydney in a nearly brand new Airbus A-380. Your mind isn't focused on the miracle of sipping champagne and finishing a canapé on a reclining leather seat 20,000 feet in the air. Instead, you're preoccupied with work you need to complete while on the flight. You appreciate the extra space so you can type on your laptop and catch up with a thousand work things.

Suddenly you hear a bang. Then a second later, a louder one shakes the whole airplane. What sounds like thousands of pieces of shrapnel rattle across the fuselage. The plane lurches, then steadies. You don't panic, but you don't know what to think. You look out the window and see an engine on fire. You scan the wing anxiously and notice parts of it are missing. The hum of the plane's engines becomes inconsistent, and the plane zigzags.

You do a quick inventory of your life so far, and it comes up short. No time for regrets, but if you'd known you had such an uncertain immediate future, you'd have made a few amends and changes—not regarding your work but your loved ones. Work no longer has the same grip on you that it had seconds before.

For 440 passengers and 29 crew members of Qantas Flight 32 on November 4, 2010, this nightmare situation was reality. The inside port engine had exploded as the plane climbed out of Singapore, setting off 54 simultaneous warning messages for the cockpit crew. Focusing first on keeping the plane in the air, the captain and crew had to determine how to land it with flight control software not designed to deal with this flying configuration. In addition, the plane had no antilock brakes. The flaps and hydraulics were damaged, and the landing gear wouldn't lower. At first, the flight control computer was unable to calculate the landing distance required. On the second try, it indicated the plane needed all but the last 100 meters of the runway, provided the crew could fly the crippled plane precisely and at the exact speed needed to touch down safely.

As a passenger in that plane, would you prefer the pilot and crew didn't panic but remain truly calm and focused?

In his book *QF32*, Captain Richard de Crespigny describes how he managed this crisis. The situation was so complex that the safe landing of the airplane and survival of all passengers and crew has been described as a miracle.

Being calm was the prerequisite. This mental and emotional state allowed the captain and crew to focus on the *right* things and not get distracted by the *wrong* things. They could then use various processes effectively and create innovative solutions to situations they hadn't foreseen or had never before experienced.

This state is the *calm* discussed in this book. Not merely relaxation, *calm* is the ability to take the right action at the right time, even under extreme pressure. This is mindfulness at work.

All That Training But . . .

The corporate world collectively spends billions on training, including personality profiling, team building, corporate retreats, creativity conferences, counseling, coaching, getting to know yourself, getting to know others—the list is endless. Our appetite for improvement is immense, but we're still not satisfied. U.S. companies alone spend almost $14 billion annually on leadership development, yet only seven percent of senior managers think their leaders are able to effectively develop leaders for a global economy. All that training, and we're still missing the mark.

And now 'mindfulness' has taken the stage, but it *still* doesn't solve our problems. Why not? Because our business lives are dependent on action, not just contemplation. Although mindfulness can help us calm down, see the big picture and quiet some of the noise, being in business requires that we *do* something. Yes, we're expected to produce something. Our performance will be measured by finite results.

The concept of mindfulness is currently being used in business without much clarity around its meaning. The term seems deliberately loose and vague, expressed in such phrases as 'a sense of being', 'a happy feeling', 'a sense of peace', or 'a heightened awareness'. Yet mindfulness can be too easily shattered as soon as we get back to work.

Define Mindfulness

Mindfulness is about our thinking: being aware of our thinking, sensing when it leads us astray, knowing when we're on the right path. We're doing the *right* thing, not just doing things *right*. After all, aren't we paid to do clear thinking?

A Definition:

Mindfulness is being aware of your thinking and its impact on both yourself and others.

As the story of Qantas Flight 32 demonstrates, being calm is the prerequisite to clear thinking. So achieving a sense of calm even under pressure becomes the goal.

Honestly, most of us can use more calm in our lives, but many of us find it difficult to be in a calm state even when we're expected to be—for example, when we're on vacation. We may seem outwardly calm but, internally we're in turmoil. How could we possibly perform at our best without a sense of calm?

We have real issues in our lives that need to be addressed, and they don't magically go away when we sit still in meditation to become calm. These issues involve work pressures, money, relationships, health—and they all need to be addressed. It would seem to be easy to be calm when we've put these issues aside, but how can we put them aside? How is it possible to stay mindful even under all the pressures of work and life in general? More than that, how can we act mindfully at *all* times?

When faced with his QF32 crisis, Captain de Crespigny didn't have time to enjoy a 10-minute meditation nor engage in a two-minute focused breathing exercise. Similarly, we can't call a time-out during a tense business meeting, go to a quiet room, and come back ten minutes later. We have to respond *immediately* to what's in front of us, but in a mindful way.

Business has always been about results, whether it concerns profitability or other more nebulous measures. That pressure, to constantly thrive in a business environment and always deliver results, never goes away. We don't get results by sitting still.

An Approach to Finding the Root Cause of Issues

Captain de Crespigny had to uncover the underlying cause producing those 54 warning messages so he could land the plane safely. He couldn't rely on the warning messages themselves: there were too many to deal with and most of them were misleading. He had to remain calm. How can you learn to do that, too?

The CALM™ approach—the subject of this book—addresses four key stages of achieving and maintaining calm. It starts with finding the root cause of issues. If we don't address the cause, the issues will keep coming back. Sound familiar?

For us, the root cause of our business issues always relates to the way we think. If we don't understand our underlying thinking, it will be difficult to change situations or resolve issues.

There is growing agreement on this point, as evidenced by this report from McKinsey:

> Looking inward is a way to examine your own modes of operating to learn what makes you tick. Individuals have their own inner lives, populated by their beliefs, priorities, aspirations, values, and fears. These interior elements vary from one person to the next, directing people to take different actions.
>
> Interestingly, many people aren't aware that the choices they make are extensions of the reality that operates in their hearts and minds. Indeed, you can live your whole life without understanding the inner dynamics that drive what you do and say. Yet it's crucial that those who seek to lead powerfully and effectively look at their internal experiences, precisely because they direct how you take action, whether you know it or not. Taking accountability as a leader today includes understanding your motivations and other inner drives.[1]

Uncover Our Thinking

Yes, understanding how we think is crucial, and once we uncover its power, change becomes surprisingly easy. Thus, it's time to address the

---

1   Nate Boaz and Erica Ariel Fox, "Change Leader, Change Thyself," McKinsey Quarterly, March 2014.

following three aspects of our thinking:

1. **The underlying principles of how we think.** Almost every approach, mindful or not, treats thought as something to be dealt with as necessary when it arises. We're generally not told how we came up with the thought in the first place. This book explains clearly and logically how we are truly the authors of our own experience.

2. **How to change our thinking.** Change is all about letting go so our innate intelligence can shine through. It's not about doing *more* thinking; it's about accessing the *right* thinking.

3. **How to stay in that mindful place.** How can we hang out there even when we're working? This book explains the surprising impact of mood, both individual and collective, on an organization's performance, and the benefit for everyone of maintaining a calm, mindful state.

The Origins of the CALM Approach

I was not always calm. Born with a 'nervous disposition' that showed up as a drive to succeed and a focus on detail, I wanted to ensure nothing 'untoward' happened. Although these were useful attributes in my early career at IBM and other computer companies, I then moved into management consulting. In this field I discovered something interesting and useful: If I was calm, then others around me became calm too, and we could make great progress. Once we were given a little time and space to examine the problems at hand, answers that first seemed intractable became obvious and clear. It seemed the more I focused on being calm and helping the client find clarity, and the less on my detailed analysis, the more successful the assignments were.

Intrigued, I decided to investigate further. So I asked, "If the benefits of being calm were so clear, what would happen if we became even calmer?" For me, this thought initiated a decades-long search for deeper peace and calm through following traditional mindfulness practices, especially meditation.

My Being was Calm—Finally

I finally reached a point in which my being was calm, in fact it was extremely calm... almost too calm. I had come to the end of a 10-day silent meditation retreat. I had risen at 4:30 a.m. every morning and either meditated or rested all day. I had predominantly meditated free of contact with anyone. It was just me, trying not to think.

How hard was it? Let me draw comparisons from my life. Specifically, I had ski-toured across the European Alps and on many occasions slipping would have meant a rapid vertical descent of 1,000 meters (landing on rocks at the bottom). I'd been arrested and detained at a Turkish border checkpoint (I'd watched a movie about this called *Midnight Express* a year earlier so I was especially scared). I'd stolen a flag from the headquarters of the Revolutionary Guard in Iran (and still I tell my children to be especially sensible!). I'd sailed in two Fastnet yachting races (but only completed one because our yacht started sinking in the other), and I completed an ironman triathlon—swim, cycle, and *then* run a marathon. I also gave the kiss of life to a man we had rescued in a storm in the English Channel (though unlike a movie's Hollywood ending, he couldn't be revived).

Despite all of these hair-raising adventures, the silent meditation retreat was the most difficult thing I'd ever done. I sat still, alone, with nothing but my thoughts. For many people, that is their worst fear: To find out who they truly are—just as I did during that retreat.

Find Our True Nature

It takes a while for our minds to calm down, to let the buzz of our constant thinking die away, to allow our innate, peace-seeking nature to shine through. When freed from chasing our thoughts, we'll find our true nature is one of completeness, wholeness, and innate health. *We are an integral part of everything.*

Yes, the enlightenment experience I'd been chasing had occurred. And much more. My thinking had been freed and went to all sorts of magical places. As my mentor, Bob Adamson, said when we talked about this, "The mind is highly creative. No wonder you experienced all sorts of things sitting still for ten days".

When my retreat was over, it was time to speak again, but I had nothing to say. In the car, returning to the city, everything looked vivid, bright, and new to me. But the people we passed—all of them—looked burdened, so burdened by their thoughts. It was as if they were weighed down by heavy wet burlap sacks full of memories, hopes, and fears, while I felt light and free. I knew I could live the monastic life and stay light and unconcerned. My experiences could only get better!

But I also knew my place was back in the world of family, friends, and work.

Achieving the Impossible

And what work it was—fast paced, pressured—with big projects and tight deadlines for global IT companies, seemingly achieving the impossible time after time. My cadre of fellow project managers lived with pressure and stress as a daily occurence, and one by one they succumbed to its effects. We joked at IBM that this acronym stood for "I've Been Married," but that was too close to the truth to be a good joke!

In this pressure cooker, I kept working while still recalling the peace and calm of my meditative practices. However, slowly I became overwhelmed. I questioned whether what I'd learned was the truth after all. For something to be true, it needed to be true all the time and in all situations. That meant it had to be as valid in the workplace as on the retreat.

Mindfulness practices did seem to offer a quick respite, a slice of peace here and there. But work seemed crazy. It was as if I had one set of thoughts when I was resting in mindfulness and another rigid, frantic and rushed set when I was working. My colleagues and I talked about work-life balance this way: work is onerous, stressful, and frantic, while life is recovering from it—only to return to the craziness each Monday. Most unsatisfactory!

The Three Principles of Mind, Thought, and Consciousness

Fortunately I then came across something that seemed too incredible to be true. It continues to be incredible to this day—except now it makes inherent sense.

I discovered a secular, logical explanation of mindfulness called the *Three Principles of Mind, Thought, and Consciousness*.[2] These underlying principles explain how we experience the world, why we do what we do, and why others do what they do. They represent the logic of the psyche, or to be more precise, the underlying principles of psychology. The answer I was seeking was not in the world of mysticism; it was back in the world of the first practice I had used to explore our mental world—psychology.

I felt determined to see if these Three Principles worked in the workplace - and they did!

A project is a microcosm of an organization, with virtually every function replicated on a smaller, more-understandable scale. Each project provides an open laboratory in which we can see what works and what doesn't, with all activities contributing to a measurable goal. Each project is full of stress, opportunities for mistrust, miscommunication, and outright organized resistance.

I tried these principles while running my projects, and we learned we could turn around any troubled project in three weeks to meet its original timeframe, scope, and budget. These principles—based on identifying the underlying thinking that causes any issue—lend themselves to practical and profoundly effective ways to address these issues through mindfulness.

---

2   Sydney Banks, The Missing Link: Reflections on Philosophy & Spirit, International Human Relations Consultants Inc., 1998

But you might say "Surely changing thinking is the hardest thing in the world". No, it actually isn't hard to change thinking—that is, not if you know how you created a thought in the first place.

Inspired by this train of thought, I developed, tested, shared, and finally created the CALM approach. The concepts of Practical Mindfulness™ draw on the experience of many business consultants who operate from an understanding of these principles. In particular, Alexander Caillet of the Accompli group introduced me to many of the exercises in this book, and he graciously allows me to use them. We both have the same view: the more people understand how their thinking affects everything they do, the better place the world will be.

Deeply Practical Book

You'll find this deeply practical book is filled with information about how to become and *remain* mindful in your working life.

The book is divided into two parts:

1. The CALM Approach itself
2. Practical, Business-Oriented Applications

Here's what you'll discover in each chapter:

Chapter 1: For Goodness Sake, CALM DOWN!

In this chapter, I tell the story of a pre-CALM business failure and how I discovered the Three Principles that gave me the key to preventing such failures in the future. I discuss what it means to calm down, why that's useful, and how we can do this easily.

Chapter 2: Find the Root CAUSE

You're calm and that's great. But now what? The point in business is to do something and do it mindfully. First, you need to find the root cause of an issue, because if you don't, the issue will return again and again. And yes, the first great secret is that the root cause of any issue is our thinking. In this chapter, you'll discover approaches and techniques (including our Insight Generator) to not only find the root cause of an issue, but also the underlying thinking and 'reinforcers' that created it.

Chapter 3: Be AWARE of How You Think

The second great secret is this: you are the author of your experience—which means, of course, you are the only person who can change it. However, if you want to change your thinking, you first need to know how it works. In this chapter you'll go deeper into the Three Principles and explore how you use them to create your experience as a unique human being.

Chapter 4: LET It Go

The third great secret is this: accessing insight and wisdom requires that you deliberately *not* think. The key is to let go of what's bothering you and allow your innate wisdom and insight to do the rest. How? *Get listened to.*

Chapter 4 goes more deeply into this critical aspect of becoming calm and clear. You'll learn how to perform this important act—to *really* listen to someone.

Chapter 5: Get in the Right MOOD

This chapter reveals the fourth great secret: rather than focus on your thinking, you want to focus on your *mood*.

Typically, we're taught in business that emotions should be discounted, controlled, or ignored altogether, yet when using the CALM approach, they're the *key* to staying mindful at all times. Our basic experience is that of living in the feeling of our thinking.

Check out the powerful relationship between mood and mindset. Using the Mood Mapper in this chapter, you'll see how your own mood has a powerful effect on others. You'll discover how far you can cast your shadow—and your light.

The remaining chapters show you how to apply the CALM approach to typical—and until now often intractable—business problems.

Chapter 6: Less Stress, More Success

Once you get going, it's good to *keep* going. This chapter helps you understand the true causes of stress and why it benefits you to minimize them. You'll discover how to access your innate resilience to see you through any situation.

Chapter 7: Too Busy To Think Straight

I could share any number of amazing time management techniques with you, but until you address the fundamental belief that you *have* to be busy, you are just going to become frantic again. We use the CALM approach to discover that less is indeed more.

Chapter 8: From There to Here

Unlock the secret to getting things done in your organization by being and acting mindfully. Help everyone become clear about exactly what the future holds.

Chapter 9: Clarity and Ownership

You can present details and processes until your eyes cross. But in any project, people have to know what is theirs to do and take ownership to do it. They also require the time and space to work it out for themselves rather than be told what to do. This chapter explains the key to clarity and getting things done: ownership.

Chapter 10: Transformed Meetings

If one thing dominates our work lives, it's meetings. You'll learn to understand the key to participating in a successful meeting—paying attention to the *tone*.

Chapter 11: Putting Off Procrastination

Everyone, yes everyone, has trouble at times doing what he or she is supposed to do. This chapter reveals the surprising advantages of procrastination and how to be mindful of what putting off a task tells you. You'll understand the role of thought and use the CALM approach to sort out the whole sorry mess.

Chapter 12: Pollyanna Was Right

From three simple principles—Mind, Thought, and Consciousness—a new world opens up. It may seem too good to be true, but it *is* true. Chapter 11 addresses frequently asked questions or concerns about CALM.

Once you learn how to apply these Three Principles, you'll look at your working life in a completely different light. Yes, you'll calm down, and stay calm—great!

But don't just sit there. Get ready for the most fascinating journey of your life.

PART I:

THE CALM APPROACH

CHAPTER 1
For Goodness Sake, CALM DOWN!

If you can keep your head when all about you
Are losing theirs and blaming it on you . . .

– "If" by Rudyard Kipling

Calmness, completeness. This is your innate state before your thinking gets in the way. Once you truly realize that, you'll naturally find a way to calm down. Chapter 3 discusses this concept in detail with respect to the Three Principles of Mind, Consciousness, and Thought. Here you'll start by exploring the nature of thought.

Success has many fathers; failure is an orphan

My own journey was long and difficult. Finally, I discovered how to be calm in the corporate boardroom, not just on the retreat. For me, the tipping point came with a failure.

At one point in my career I had to deal with a very public failure. I remember the feeling clearly. I had tried my best, but it wasn't good enough. The project had failed to meet its objectives and the customer had thrown us out. It is as bad as it gets, failing in a project is one thing, losing a big customer is another thing all together. We had had successes and setbacks, overcome all sorts of obstacles, but we just couldn't make the system work. I was exhausted, the team was exhausted, and we had nothing to show for all the effort we put in.

They left me alone for a little while to recover.

Needing a break, I drove along the winding roads above the city. I stopped at my favorite place, an old house at the summit of the range. Sitting there and looking down over the city, I felt a sense of distance. I watched the hustle and bustle below, but I was alone and separate from it. I tried to make sense of it all. But no matter how I looked at it, I felt I'd failed, and failed in public, and being the project manager, I was the natural target for blame. What was I going to do?

I had excuses. I'd taken over a 'basket case' of a project and nearly made it work. The team performed amazingly by introducing innovative processes and building strong relationships. Our issues' management was fantastic. We'd all done our best—but it wasn't good enough. The project failed. Something more was needed, but I didn't know what.

I knew from experience that calming down was a good idea. It helped get everyone working well together and making progress on the system. Yet for most of the project, I myself hadn't been calm and nor had the key decision makers. Whenever the blame lay, one thing was true: *We must have made poor decisions or we couldn't have gotten the result we did.* Because we thought the problem could be solved by working harder, we'd all thrown ourselves into the task. We honestly couldn't have worked any harder, but the result was worse than nothing!

We had missed something critical, and that rankled me. The key to effective business is making good decisions, and because decisions are based on thinking, our thinking must have been faulty.

The Green Carpet

It all began well. It was a challenge but I thrived on challenges. I remember the atmosphere, the smell, the view and the décor. I had been appointed the project director of a major new initiative, and it was already in trouble by the time I arrived. I was welcomed as a new face and the chance to put everything right. Every week I went with my senior managers to the customer's boardroom at the top of one of the tallest buildings in the city. We always took time to notice the surroundings. The view, the helipad on top of the roof, the furnishings, all reeked of power, especially the carpet. No muted tones here - it was bright green. Someone had a strong enough personality to pull off that preference.

The boardroom with the green carpet had two entrances. One started from the floor below and was guarded by an executive secretary. Visitors then walked up a wide, sweeping staircase framed in dark polished wood to the top floor. The spectacular view showcased the city, the harbor, and the ocean beyond.

I made a point of turning up early to these meetings. So did my administration manager, as well as the head of Regional Professional Services, the Country Manager, and the Asia-Pacific industry lead. We wanted to talk and make sure we had our story straight. We knew we were in big trouble in many ways. Mostly, we were in danger of missing our delivery date, plus our organization was losing a lot of money on a fixed-price contract because our costs were running out of control. The team had endured several changes of leadership in a short period of time.

I tried to calm down, but the stress was getting to me. Here I was—in this world where I spent most of my waking hours—and it was making me sick. In fact, I hadn't felt well for weeks on end. For this meeting, the customer's project sponsor, key team members, country CEO, and his boss from the region arrived using their own internal lift or elevator. We all acted civilly, but not cordially. The meeting—*my* meeting—was about to begin.

The Progression of Project Managers

Was the result my fault? I was the third Green Carpet project director. The first two had been fired. We used to joke that every project goes through four project managers. Typically, the first one starts it off full of promise and enthusiasm. For that manager, the joy of the sales cycle is fresh and life seems easy. The budget appears huge with plenty of money for team and relationship building. No problems yet. But this first project manager knows more about selling than implementing something new, which involves completely different skills.

The second project manager is a management professional. The predecessor gets out (or is let out) of the project quickly. The management professional assembles a pile of hopes, dreams, and sales assurances into a coherent plan—and then the bad news breaks. Things are not as simple as they seem. Everyone who approved the project had a different idea of what it was doing and what benefit it would bring. Each project is a unique endeavor that's never been done before, and something always goes wrong. Depending on circumstances, the second PM can sometimes overcome these problems with his or her reputation intact. If not, someone like me gets the call—the turnaround specialist.

As the third project manager, I'm like a marriage counselor. I have to quickly initiate either a fresh start or a clean break. Troubled projects are defined by troubled relationships, which are characterized by 'villainizing' (it's all *their* fault), distrust, miscommunication, and fear. The noise is so great. People can't tell what they already have and what the chances of success might be.

Managing Mindsets

For me on this Green Carpet project, the easy part was determining what we had at that particular moment. Contrary to common business belief, most troubled projects don't lack process or documentation. Most of the key documents existed, although typically the project members might not have been aware of their existence.

After a poor start, the hard part to manage was the team's mindset. Given all that had happened, I had to get participants back into a productive, working frame of mind in the midst of all the grumbling. I had to get them to focus on how to get things to happen, rather than protect themselves from things going wrong.

When I first met the team, I had been told to report to a certain location for an unspecified role. The project was kept secret, both for the commercial protocol of introducing an innovative product into the marketplace, and because it was in profound trouble. I could *taste* the frantic thinking going on. Desperate to succeed and frightened of failure, the team simply didn't know how to pull it off.

So I set to work. I listened to everyone's story, each individual strongly pointing fingers. Relationships had broken down to the point where issues had become highly personal. Mistakes had been made, sure; but these mistakes were being used to damn someone's character.

I had two imperatives. First were matters of healing and trust—that is, healing the relationships among team members, and building trust in my own management. That trust had to come from both *my* team and the *customer's* team so those involved could achieve the outcome they desperately wanted. Second was bringing order out of the chaos by introducing processes people would and could follow—in both a technical and an emotional sense.

I didn't learn this by reading business literature or taking a training course. In terms of personal relationships, courses and books build elaborate frameworks and present complex analyses, saying lots about how it should *look*, but little on how to *do* it. By then I had learned the key: *to always be calm.*

Well, we finished creating the product, sort of. It went 'live' when it did because the company had booked the advertising months in advance. However, the product itself had many problems—and ultimately, those in command threw it out. They looked at the cost of further development using the same technical approach and decided what we'd built was too clumsy and rigid to meet their needs. Failure!

No matter how detached you are, running a project with hundreds of people eats up your emotional resources until you can give no more. My team and I had done everything: implemented great processes, gotten things onto an even keel, established great teamwork, and addressed the human side of things. But all the energy and enthusiasm in the world was useless: *we weren't doing the right thing.*

So of course a fourth project manager had to replace me and tidy it up at the end.

My Awakening

After the Green Carpet project, I kept on working on projects, still gravitating towards trouble, sorting out issue after issue. At times I found the stress overwhelming. My calm evaporated and I became busy-minded. It seemed impossible in the business environment to actually *be* calm and *stay* calm.

One day, I came home from work and my wife said something that stopped me in my tracks. I'd been casually commenting on a business situation that had occurred that day, and she responded, "That's just your thinking."

We'd always made sure to take the time each day to check in and discuss the day's events. Because we were both in executive positions, the conversation did tend to get a bit involved at times. But this comment was unusual. There's something annoying about having your experience apparently discounted in such a dismissive way. I explained the situation again, to be met with the same response: "Yes, as I said, it's just your thinking."

This was serious. *I* was the one with the degree in psychology and the MBA. *I* was the one who had the interest in every theory of personality and motivation. *I* was the one who constantly studied work from a psychological viewpoint; writing papers and making presentations at international conferences. *I* was the expert, and *I knew* it was all about our thinking. But *just* my thinking? Though quite annoyed, I was also intrigued.

"Here" she added, "read this article: The Principles Revisited [3] It talked about being calm, but it also talked about something else.

So of course I read it, and it went on and on about this marvelous thing

---

[3] This document has been revised (revisited) many times by the author, Judy Sedgeman. It is available on her website: www.three-principles.com

called the Three Principles. Everything made perfect, logical sense—that is, all of our experience is based on the Three Principles of Mind, Thought, and Consciousness. It was about how the way in which we use them together creates our unique view of the world.

So big deal, what was the fuss all about?

Well, for one thing, my wife had changed. She was still the same person I fell in love with and married all those years ago, and who I am still married to today. But she was calmer, happier. She seemed to have a different view on life than before, and she lived it from a more centered, profound core. She was . . . well . . . more *herself*.

Later, I met other people who were grounded in the Three Principles. They were excited by the potential unleashed by a better understanding of how we function as human beings. They also seemed normal—the most normal people you could ever meet. Not dull, not resigned, but in touch with something fundamental and true. They were calm but not passive. They were somehow always in the present moment. They also told the most incredible stories about how people's lives had been transformed by this understanding, whether they were in prison, a housing project, involved in counseling or business. It all seemed too good to be true.

The Role of Listening

I wanted to experience more of the understanding, peace, and wisdom that came with the Three Principles. I attended courses; I read helpful essays and blog posts. I was intrigued—but I still didn't get it. I noticed something interesting though. All the people I met who worked with the Three Principles were great listeners. They didn't seem to be using any trick or technique. Rather, they had a genuine interest in what I was saying. They projected an indefinable presence that allowed me to calm down. The more I talked, the calmer I got and the better perspective I had. I discovered *I could be calm no matter what*.

You can't do this on your own. I've tried and tried all sorts of practices. I was discussing this with Toby Ouvry, a Buddhist monk, who has returned to the business world to teach calm and meditation. What he told me rang true: "The mind has a ceaseless desire to create. Left on your own, your thoughts will probably run away with you."

So there is one surefire way to calm down in any situation: get listened to by someone who truly understands how listening works and how the mind works.

You can do this three ways:

1. Seek out people who have this quality. You will know them by their presence. Inspirational leaders have this quality, but they are few and far between.

2. Find a coach who truly knows listening and the fundamental importance of this approach.

Go to www.thecalmrevolution.com and look up our directory of CALM-certified coaches. Notice they have something in common: they all mention the Three Principles. They know how to listen in a way that works.

You might think it's cheating to get help. You may want to work your issues out and become calm on your own, but that's extremely difficult. I've tried it and failed. I'm serious. Get help!

Other Ways to Become CALM

Strangely enough, once I became calm, I started investigating how other calm people did it. I discovered that traditional mindfulness practice is only one of many ways people can calm down. Rather than being an esoteric practice, calmness or mindfulness is an innate state we can return to in many different ways. For example:

- My brother-in-law is an avid windsurfer and kite-boarder. The way he describes his state of mind when he's surfing the big waves seems exactly like mindfulness to me. That's probably why he does it so much.

- My manager in PeopleSoft was also a keen surfer.

Somehow he managed to arrange it so he could get away when the surf was running. We learned to check the surf forecast for added certainty when scheduling a meeting.

- As a management consultant in London, I often went to the pub with friends after work, relaxed over a beer, and resolved the issues of the day.

- My best friend loves fishing. Five minutes from his office he has a boat ready to go. When he goes out, he's totally absorbed in the task of catching his dinner.

- Racing driver Alain Prost has reported being in a deeply calm state while hurtling around a race track as fast as a human being can go. Top performers often report being in a similar state of flow.

- The dean of a major business school reports that he swims 400 meters every morning. After the first length, he slips into a calm, mindful state.

We can do many things to become calm: sing, dine with convivial company, watch movies, dance, laugh, play a sport, ride a bicycle . . . We don't necessarily have to cease doing everything to become calm. What's important is our inner state.

When I developed the CALM™ approach, I found it instantly resonated with almost everyone I met. Being calm touches something deep and profound within almost everyone. In the end, we all want peace—that deep inner peace that enables us to be centered, authentic, and real. For me, it was not enough to *be* calm. I felt I had to use this state to take mindful action—to act compassionately no matter where I was, even at work; *especially* at work.

Issue #1: Don't Want to Be Calm

Then I encountered this issue: *Many people didn't want to be calm in the first place*. They didn't equate being calm with being productive or effective. They would proudly talk about how busy they were, how hard they had to work at certain time. While espousing slogans like "We need to work smarter, not harder" they themselves seemed to be in a permanent state of busyness and exhaustion. Life seemed to be one long series of crises and impending disasters they seemed to live by an internal mantra "Never good enough". They were always working towards some future state when finally they would be calm, once they had finished everything on their list, but never got there, because the list was always growing.

The Dalai Lama was once asked a similar question: "Your Holiness, you have devoted your life to trying to help all human beings be happy. You have been clear and consistent in your approach. You have communicated widely and always the same simple message of how to be happy. You yourself are an exemplar of that approach. Your teachings are simple and straightforward. Why is it that, despite all this, there are still so many people who will not hear?"

His Holiness replied, "It is because they prefer things as they are."

I investigated further. I found that most people were *distrustful* of being calm. They liked being constantly stimulated. Of course they did. Why else would they put so much effort and money into being constantly distracted by email, social media, online entertainment and the like? In the 17th century, Blaise Pascal famously said, "All men's miseries derive from not being able to sit in a quiet room alone." In today's connected world, we are even more challenged because our possibilities for sitting alone in a quiet room are severely limited.

In his book *Simply Managing*, Henry Mintzberg described the full-on, always energetic mental state that most managers live in:

> Over 40 studies of managerial work dating back to the 1950s show that executives "just sort of dash around all the time."
>
> . . . I noticed the work pace of the chief executives was unrelenting. They met a steady stream of callers and mail, from their arrival in the morning until their

> departure in the evening. Coffee breaks and lunches were inevitably work-related, and ever-present people in their organization were ready to usurp any free moment ... The quantity of work to be done, or at least, what managers choose to do during the day, is substantial, and, after-hours, senior managers appear to be able to escape neither from a situation that recognizes the power of their position nor from their own pre-dispositions to worry about their current problems.[4]

Anyone who has been a manager knows how immense the pressures are and how they are never-ending in nature. As soon as you complete your annual goals, you're given another set that's equally or more challenging.

Henry Mintzberg is a hero of mine because, rather than only talking about what managers *should* do, he took the time to observe what things were really like for them. Unless we understand the issues that they face we can't provide advice. He saw a life of constant interruption and unrelenting pressure. He found that, on average, they had a maximum of 20 minutes to spend on any one task.

Then he noticed something else. An initial study, by Sune Carlson, asked why chief executives didn't make better use of their assistants and delegate more work to protect themselves. Mintzberg followed this up with an observation: "[Are] brevity, variety and fragmentation forced on the managers, or do they choose this pattern in their work? My answers are yes, both times, especially the second. The five chief executives of my early study appeared to be properly protected by their secretaries, and there was no reason to believe they were inferior delegators. Instead, they sometimes preferred interruption and denied themselves free time."[5]

As the Dalai Lama said, they prefer things this way. It's the reality of working life.

I've been there, and such intensity can provide quite a buzz. Having

---

4   Henry Mintzberg, *Simply Managing: What Managers Do—and Can do Better.* Berrett-Koehler Publishers, 2013. p. 18.

5   Ibid. p. 20.

a mind that's fully turned on and operating energetically can be highly enjoyable. But you can't keep it up forever. And lost in the genius of your own thinking, there's not much room for the ideas of others. (Chapter 5 graphically depicts the effect of this busy-mindedness by leaders on an organization's overall performance.)

Issue #2: I Don't Know How to Be Calm

The second issue I uncovered was that people simply didn't believe they could be calm in a typical work environment. They'd never experienced it and thought they never would. But it can be attained by being in the presence of someone who's calm. In my professional talks, this is where we go right away. What a heady experience being in a room with hundreds of people and all of them are in a calm, thoughtful state. But in many organizations, rarely is anyone in this state, nor is it encouraged.

What does it mean to be calm? Calm is our innate state *before* we start thinking.

Notice I said *innate*, not *normal*. No doubt most people's "normal" state is buzzing with a constant stream of thoughts—a running commentary on what's happening, what should happen, what they're doing and what others should be doing - a constant energetic barrage of thoughts.

But consider this. What would happen if you stopped thinking for just a little bit and quieted that commentary to a murmur?

Well, for starters you'd discover the world carries on as it always has, unaffected by your perception of it.

Next, you'd find you're doing pretty much the same things you've been doing all along, minus the distracting commentary.

Finally, you'd experience moments of mental quiet, more inner space, and a lot more perspective. You'd see things as they really are, not how you think they should be.

From an early age we've been taught that thinking is the key—that we can solve our problems by thinking *more*. When I joined IBM as a graduate trainee, the company's motto was simply "Think." We thought we could think our way out of any situation.

But to find calm, you have to *let go* of your thinking and think *less*. Again, calm is your innate state—before you grab hold of your thoughts. Because it's innate, you'll always be able to find calm inside of you as part of your core, your soul. Once you accept its innate nature, you'll discover a way to experience it.

For an example of this, meet Gavin Ingram. Gavin is a calm, enthusiastic guy who exudes the simple, clear nature of mindfulness. He's able to see opportunities where others see obstacles.

Dealing with What Is

Gavin Ingram is Legal Director Asia of AdventBalance, one of the fastest growing secondment law firms in Australia and Asia. AdventBalance was established in 2008 and currently has offices throughout Australia, as well as in Singapore and Hong Kong.

AdventBalance's unique and innovative business model features all of its lawyers and consultants working from their clients' premises. Gavin explains, "The traditional law firm model is based on extremely high fixed costs such as office space, client reception floors, artwork, baristas, partner car parks, and the latest and greatest electronic gadgets. To pay for those overheads, law firms are forced to charge extremely high rates for what is often day-to-day legal work. Because at AdventBalance all of our lawyers sit with our clients, we have been able to strip out all those non-value-adding overheads and reduce legal spend for clients. Sitting with the client and becoming a part of the client allows our lawyers to add *more* value, given they are part of the action and can contribute to a broader range of matters. They can see and hear what is happening while looking for ways things can be done better. Our lawyers get to know our client's business very well. Therefore, they can quickly give responsive, practical, and commercial advice."

I comment, "I've discussed your model with other lawyers, and they wonder how you maintain control over quality, let alone know whether your lawyers are working hard or not."

Gavin responds, "To do this, you must have strict criteria when it comes to hiring lawyers. You need lawyers who are well trained, have good in-house experience, and are a good cultural fit. Cultural fit is very important given the lawyer is working directly with the client. The lawyers have to get on well with the people they're working with. They also need to have higher levels of EQ. We look for lawyers who are well credentialed and have a track record of success.

Our unique model appeals to high-level lawyers as we provide flexibility in how they work and rich variety in terms of the type of work they can do. We have a large number of female lawyers working for us. That's because we can offer, for example, flexibility for working moms when they need it. Many of them have young families, so they might want to work only in the mornings when their children are in school or child care. They may want to take time off for school holidays.

In addition, some of our lawyers only want to work part of the year; they value flexibility over everything else. We also find they're extremely productive given they are solely focused on working for one client at any one time. Our lawyers are always fresh and highly motivated. Often, they take advantage of the flexible work environment and recharge their batteries between assignments."

Gavin adds, "A lot of lawyers are interested in working for us. They have hit a point in their careers where having interests outside of work and achieving more balance in their lives becomes important. Working for a top law firm requires extremely long hours in an ultra-competitive environment. The expectation and pressure to bill are immense. After all, those fixed costs need to be covered!

"Unfortunately, lawyers often have to sacrifice personal life to meet targets and stay ahead of all the other lawyers vying for the limited partner appointments. Don't get me wrong; the work undertaken by lawyers in top law firms and the experience can be exciting and rewarding. Lawyers get paid well for the sacrifices they make. At the end of the day, the clients pay very high fees, which largely end up in the pockets of the partners to pay off the fixed overheads."

I ask, "Are your *clients* open to flexible working hours if you have a lawyer who only wants to work half days?"

Gavin replies, "Our clients are open and supportive of flexible in-sourcing of legal services. The secret is always putting the very best lawyer forward for the role. We never compromise on that. Once you put the best lawyer forward, clients will often be accommodating to make sure the secondment works for them and the lawyer."

Finally I ask, "Are innovative and alternative legal

service providers a threat to the traditional law firm?"

Gavin replies, "There will always be demand and a place for traditional law firms. What we will see and are currently seeing is general counsel actively seeking more cost-effective, value-added solutions for day-to-day legal services. The deep expertise of the traditional law firm will still be required for complex legal work requiring experts in their field. For example, spending $1,000 an hour on legal advice may be palatable if it, in turn, reduces exposure and risk by millions of dollars. But day-to-day legal work isn't always in the context of millions of dollars of risk or outcomes. It is often just that—day-to-day legal work. Such work is better undertaken at reasonable rates by lawyers who also bring their industry knowledge and commercial expertise.

"Everybody wins in this model. Clients get access to top-flight legal advice immediately. We provide great value. Our overheads are only sixty percent of those of a traditional firm. Our staff gets something each person values greatly: flexibility. We get great lawyers who love working for us.

"The traditional model of running a law firm has been under pressure for a long time. When you focus on what *customers* want rather than what the *partners* want, you find lots of opportunities to do things in a truly innovative way that, ironically, is just common sense."

The CALM Approach

I started to see how the Three Principles could be applied in the business situations where we work. Applying them opened the door to insight, which helped us identify the root cause of business issues, identify creative solutions, and maintain a productive mindset.

What exactly is the CALM approach? First you allow yourself to be calm, which is a lot easier than you may think. You are only one thought away; and it helps if those around you are calm too. Then you work through issues using these CALM stages:

1. Find the *root cause* of the issue, which is always your thinking.
2. Become *aware* of how your thinking works.
3. *Let go* of the thinking that is the issue.
4. Let your *mood* be your guide.

Read on for a full explanation of these four secrets. You'll start with Chapter 2 which addresses the first step, finding the root cause—the C in CALM.

CHAPTER 2
Find the Root CAUSE

We can't solve problems by using the same kind of thinking we used when we created them.

- Albert Einstein

Why find the root cause? Because it's little use asking you to be calm if there is something on your mind. Why not fix that issue first, by finding out the real cause? Then we will have a little more mental time and space to explore things. This will also provide a bit more of an insight into the role of thought in creating your experience. If not, being able to find the root cause of your issues is still going to make your life run a bit smoother.

You may be thinking that because I was in charge of a failed project it hurt my career, but this wasn't the case. Thomas J. Watson Jr, founder of IBM, was quoted as saying, *"Recently, I was asked if I was going to fire an employee who made a mistake that cost the company $600,000. No, I replied, I just spent $600,000 training him."* On the Green Carpet project, we lost considerably more than that, but the principle still applies.

The saying "You are only as good as your last project" is simply not true. We all learn from our mistakes. Any successful business career is littered with projects that didn't go well - read Steve Jobs' biography. The key is what you *learn* from your mistakes. Any project manager who says he or she has never been in charge of a disaster has either not done much or is lying. No project managers would survive if we insisted on constant unbridled success.

I had gained valuable experience, as had my team. I went on to run larger, more complicated projects and rescue those in trouble. I never again wanted to go through an experience in which I hadn't ensured we were doing the right thing. I became alert to the warning signs; I would summon the courage and endure the short-term pain of taking an up-front stand if something didn't seem right. I knew I'd be avoiding even greater pain that would follow if we charged ahead anyway.

The customer of that original failed project respected the way I'd worked and used me again in other initiatives. Another plus was that as project team members, we had forged deep links with each other that I have maintained to this day.

What Was Learned?

Whenever I interviewed for a new position, I was always asked, "What have you learned?", referring to my failed project. My answer at the time was this: "You can get a team performing to the highest possible level relatively easily. If you understand people are intrinsically motivated and tap into that, your team members will aim their energy at making things work rather than defending their position. People *want* to work together. Given the right leadership, team members will work hard and even sacrifice their personal lives and relationships in pursuit of a common goal. But if you don't identify and address the root cause of an issue, you are doomed to failure."

I wish I'd known then what I know now. Any relationship can be repaired or issue resolved when you have the courage to call it out. As pointed out earlier, if you don't address the root cause of an issue, it will keep coming back.

Does that advice sound like any self-improvement programs you've tried?

Often, these programs don't address the root cause, so the results don't last and the problem stubbornly resurfaces again and again. A McKinsey report issued at the start of 2014 on why leadership training often fails states this:

> "Becoming a more effective leader often requires changing behavior. But although most companies recognize that this also means adjusting underlying mindsets, too often these organizations are reluctant to address the root causes of why leaders act the way they do." The report adds, "Identifying some of the deepest, 'below the surface' thoughts, feelings, assumptions, and beliefs is usually a precondition of behavioral change—one too often shirked in development programs."[6]

For the Green Carpet project, if we'd had this tool called the Insight Generator that follows below, we would have easily identified the root cause and probably taken the right action. However, by the time I'd taken over the project, it had triggered 36 out of 45 indicators of a troubled project. We thought we weren't working hard enough and weren't organized enough. That's the conclusion everyone usually jumps to—but it's wrong. The symptoms never reveal the source because the secret is this: *The root cause of any issue is our thinking.*

However, this secret, like the other great secrets, can't be told in any given situation because you actually can't *tell* people anything. Instead, you can only set the conditions by which they can work things out for themselves.

The calmer we are in this, the better.

Insight Generator Exercise

Let's see how the concept of Practical Mindfulness works using the Insight Generator to discover the underlying thinking or root cause of any issue.

---

6   McKinsey Quarterly, 2014 No 1 http://www.mckinsey.com/insights/leading_in_the_21st_century/why_leadership-development_programs_fail

Below is a form you may photocopy, or you can go to www.thecalmrevolution.com to download a full-size, full-color copy.

Ready? Your first task is to calm down. Find a quiet space and relax. Perhaps you can find a good listener to help you fill out the form. If you can't find a listener, go to www.thecalmrevolution.com There's a video there where I personally guide you through using this tool. The listener should ask the questions and then just listen. As the responder, you write down the answers on the form. Yes, you must write them down yourself.

Here are the steps:

> **Step 1:** In the shaded area at the top right that says 'Issue', type in your issue. It can be anything: Lack of Money, Stress, Health, Meetings, Strategy, Sales Target . . .
>
> **Step 2:** In the 'Current/Future' box, cross out 'Future'. We'll deal with the current situation first.
>
> **Step 3:** In the section next to 'Results' headed by 'We Produce', 'We Deliver', etc., write in the results you're currently experiencing in this area. Use the titles as prompts or ideas. Results are things produced, delivered, achieved, or accomplished. For example: progress against a sales target or project plan, financial goals. They are not how you feel, even though that is how the problem may reveal itself, as in "we feel bad, demoralised, disengaged" We deal with feelings later
>
> **Step 4:** In the 'Behaviors' section, write down what behaviors are producing your result. For example, you may not be making as many calls as your sales plan dictates, or your team may not be doing what they ae required to do.

Chapter 2: Find The Root CAUSE 39

The Insight Generator™

ISSUE

CURRENT / FUTURE

Results — We Produce... We Deliver... We Achieve... We Accomplish...

Behaviors — We Act Like... We Behave Like... We Manifest... We Do...

Feelings — We Feel... Our Emotions are... The Atmosphere Is...

Thinking — We Believe... Our Assumptions Are... Our Reasoning Is...

Reinforcers — Policies... Culture... Environment... Expectations....

calm

www.thecalmrevolution.com   Based on the exercise "The Thinking Path" by the Accompli Group

Step 5: In the 'Feelings' section, write down the feelings or emotions associated with those behaviors. Use the prompts: 'We Feel', 'Our Emotions are', 'The Atmosphere is' . . .

Step 6: In the 'Thinking' section, write down the thinking associated with the feelings: 'We Believe', 'Our Assumptions are, Our Reasoning is' . . .

Step 7: In the 'Reinforcers' section, write down what things reinforce the thinking. In a business environment, these might include the organization's strategy and values, organizational structure, processes and technology, leadership and people, or HR systems. For a personal issue, reinforcers might be friends, family, peer pressure, or societal norms.

It should be apparent that your results come directly from your behavior, which in turn results from how you feel, and which directly results from your thinking.
A large number of reinforcers serve to keep you thinking that way, not the least of which is the human tendency to habitually think the same way.

Would you like a different result than what you're getting? Then take another copy of the form, put in the same issue, cross out the word 'Current', and let's look into the 'Future'.

Follow the same steps, starting with the thinking, moving up through the feelings and behaviors, and ending with the results. If you have a problem with the thinking, look back at the first sheet and write down the opposite of what you wrote there.

Finally, determine what reinforcers would encourage you to think in the new way. Then sit back and answer these questions:

- What did you notice about working in the future

view where, compared with the current view, the underlying thinking was more helpful?

- At what level is it easiest to change things: the results, the behaviors, or the underlying thinking?

Personal Example

Let's look at a real example. The following case examines a person's health in a stressful job. The first page works through the current reality; the next works with the desired future state:

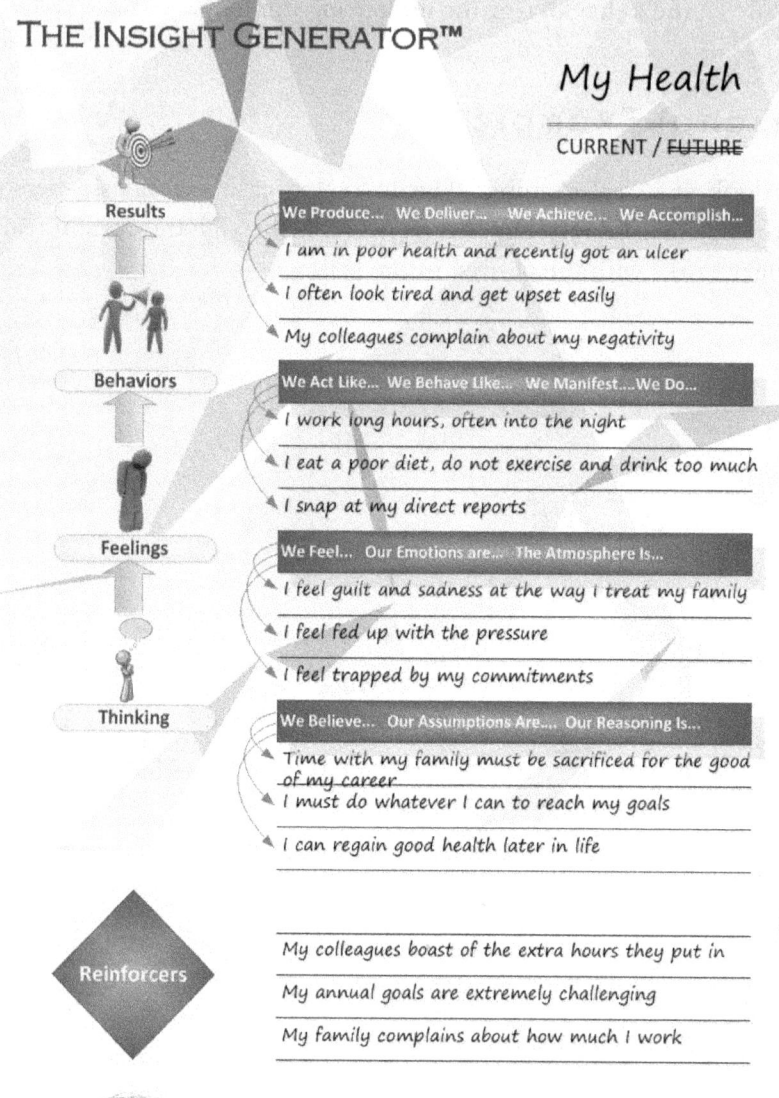

The Insight Generator™

My Health

~~CURRENT~~ / FUTURE

Results
- We Produce... We Deliver... We Achieve... We Accomplish...
- I receive excellent health check ups
- I radiate a healthy glow and shpw up relaxed
- My colleagues enjoy working with me

Behaviors
- We Act Like... We Behave Like... We Manifest....We Do...
- I know when to tale time off to be with my family
- I eat well and exercise regularly
- I request and receive support from my colleagues

Feelings
- We Feel... Our Emotions are... The Atmosphere Is...
- I feel a sense of work and life being in balance
- I feel grateful for the support I receive in all the circles in my life
- I am in control

Thinking
- We Believe... Our Assumptions Are.... Our Reasoning Is...
- Time with my family is a priority
- I will do the best to reach my goals, but not at the expense of my health, family or colleagues
- Staying healthy is the key to a good life

Reinforcers
- I refer to the corporate value: "keeping work and life in balance is the key to the success of our associates"
- My annual goals are mutually agreed upon
- My family thanks me for my contribution

www.thecalmrevolution.com   Based on the exercise "The Thinking Path" by the Accompli Group

What about work?

In business, you are often judged primarily by your results, which isn't necessarily a bad thing. After all, results indicate if something has worked. Results reinforce the discipline of focusing on what is important.

The problem is, focusing on results *for their own sake* doesn't help you achieve anything because you can't *manage* a result. Rather, a result stems from something else: people's behavior. To make a sale, your customer has to buy your product, and you have to do something to sell it.

Even managing behavior is difficult

It seems logical to focus on behavior, but this has its own difficulties: there are so many to choose from. In a recent reprint of McKinsey Managing Director Alan Bower's seminal book *The Will to Lead*, 14 key competencies or behaviors are identified as being essential for good leadership:

- Trustworthiness
- Fairness
- Unassuming behavior
- Leaders listen
- Open-mindedness
- Sensitivity to people
- Sensitivity to situations
- Initiative, initiative, initiative
- Good judgment
- Broad-mindedness
- Flexibility and adaptability
- The capacity to make good and timely decisions

- The capacity to motivate
- A sense of urgency

That is a long list. But knowing *what* to do and *doing it* are two different things. We may all agree that the behaviors described above very desirable. However, just being aware of them is not enough. In any given situation, some of them are appropriate, but others aren't. How do we tell? We need some insight, some deeper awareness, in the moment to know what to do. To make a lasting change we need to address the underlying thinking. Like losing weight, we have to eat less or differently *and* we have to exercise. But does everyone who wants to lose weight *do* that? No.

Human beings are complicated. We think and feel. We're emotional, insightful, curious beings. To change our behavior seems to be quite difficult because we're such creatures of habit. So if we want significant, noticeable change, we have to address the root cause of our behavior, our underlying assumptions, and our beliefs.

Business Example

Let's use the Insight Generator to look at a business example of an organization that has difficulty getting things done. The traditional approach is behavioral in nature, but this stirs the pot.

The Insight Generator™

Lack of Progress
CURRENT / ~~FUTURE~~

Results

We Produce... We Deliver... We Achieve... We Accomplish...
- Pace of change is slow
- Work products are not of good quality
- Problems never get fixed

Behaviors

We Act Like... We Behave Like... We Manifest....We Do...
- We don't take on new things
- Endless meetings with lots of people that don't get results
- Busy dealing with fires

Feelings

We Feel... Our Emotions are... The Atmosphere Is...
- Too busy, frustration with ongoing issues
- Our voice is not heard
- It's not worth trying anything new here

Thinking

We Believe... Our Assumptions Are... Our Reasoning Is...
- Things never get done here, so why should I try
- Don't stick your head up
- Someone else has to come and fix this
- It's all the fault of management

Reinforcers
- New initiatives from staff are rejected
- People are criticised for lack of ability
- Pressure is always on to fix short-term issues

www.thecalmrevolution.com   Based on the exercise "The Thinking Path" by the Accompli Group

When we deal with issues at the results level, we generally equate lack of progress with lack of energy and assume we're not working hard enough. We think we need motivation! Consequently, we reinforce the need for results and increase the pressure. But that produces the opposite result of what we want. It is like driving a car while pressing both the accelerator and the brake pedal at the same time.

Increasing the energy level means we will get what we already have, but we're using more effort. The energy affects both our motivators and our restraints equally.

If we look at the behavioral level, we have a few more insights into what's going on. Our meetings aren't effective, so we look at ways of running them better. We encourage people to take the initiative. We put out a few fires, though this still has limited effect.

Only when we look *deeper* do we make progress. If people feel the way they do, trying to make them act the opposite way will encourage resistance, especially passive resistance. If they genuinely feel there's no point in trying, they'll go through the motions, but little will happen.

When we get to the heart of the matter—the thinking displayed by those in the organization—we see the real problem. So how on earth do we change that? Well, for a start, we look at the messages sent out by the reinforcers, aka the managers (whether those messages are openly stated or tacit).

Thinking Our Way Up and Out

Let's turn the Insight Generator on its head and see if we can think our way up and out. First the reinforcers: Let's assume the *opposite* thinking and see where it gets us . . .

The Insight Generator™

Lack of Progress

~~CURRENT~~ / FUTURE

Results

We Produce... We Deliver... We Achieve... We Accomplish...

- Pace of change is rapid
- Work products are of good quality
- Problems don't last long

Behaviors

We Act Like... We Behave Like... We Manifest....We Do...

- We do lots of new things
- Meetings are focussed with actions that are immediate
- Busy fixing long term issues

Feelings

We Feel... Our Emotions are... The Atmosphere is...

- Busy, but we accomplish lots
- Our voice is heard and respected
- We can cope

Thinking

We Believe... Our Assumptions Are... Our Reasoning Is...

- Things get done around here, so I will pull my weight
- Call out problems **and** their solutions
- We can fix this
- Management can help sort this out

Reinforcers

- New initiatives from staff are welcomed
- People are praised for coming up with solutions
- Pressure is always on to find the root cause

www.thecalmrevolution.com   Based on the exercise "The Thinking Path" by the Accompli Group

Applying solutions at the results level is nearly always doomed to failure. Addressing behaviors is a start but is still insufficient to sustain change. Only when we go to the level of *thought* and *feeling* can we make significant progress.

But hang on a second. Isn't changing people's thinking hard, the hardest thing of all? It is *if* you don't know how thinking works. However, if you *do* know, then everything becomes easier.

To recap: First, you calm down. Then, you look for underlying thinking using the Insight Generator. Next, be aware of how people create their experience so you can fully address their thinking. Chapter 3 discusses this part of the process.

CHAPTER 3
Be AWARE of How You Think

I have deep faith that the principle of the universe will be beautiful and simple.

— Albert Einstein

The way to true calm and inner peace, no matter where we are, is to understand that calm and peace is our true nature—until our thinking gets in the way.

The road to changing our thinking so we can access this innate mental health is to understand how we think in the first place. This may seem like a strange proposition. In all of my investigation into psychology, philosophy, theology, and management thinking, I had never come across an investigation of thought itself. It is accepted as a done deal. "Thought is real. Deal with it as best you can."

Most of us have never been challenged to investigate the nature of thought itself. But mindfulness invites us to do just this, to investigate the nature of thought and our existence. Traditional mindfulness practice gives us a clue: Eastern philosophies start with mind and invite us to observe our thinking arising out of it. Western thinking is centered on the apparent reality that mind arises in the brain, and is the product of our thoughts. Eastern philosophy is centered on mind being greater than ourselves. Western thinking tends to limit the mind to what thoughts we have just at the moment.

I knew deep down that the answers I sought to both personal and business issues must lie outside of accepted thinking. You probably have the same feeling, that nothing you have heard so far truly hits the spot. As my interest in the Three Principles developed, I asked my mentors the best way to further develop my understanding. They all said, "Go and meet Sydney Banks." Thus I found myself in a conference room overlooking the surf on the north shore of Oahu, Hawaii—possibly the most beautiful spot in the world—attending a seminar hosted by Syd himself.

I had first met Syd in the elevator; we were both staying on the same floor of the hotel. When I bumped into him in the hallway, there was no profound conversation, electrical sparks, or heavenly hum. He seemed ordinary—no aura, no healing touch, no mystique. How reassuring. We've heard of spiritual teachers who abuse their powers, so we've become rightfully cautious about committing our mental well-being to someone who demands we give away our possessions and more.

Nothing close to that ever happened with Syd. In fact, he counseled *against* this tendency. As he wrote in his book, *The Missing Link*, "There is an enormous difference between finding your own inner wisdom and adopting someone else's beliefs ... Any good teacher will tell you never to be a follower. A wise teacher will draw out your innate knowledge."[7]

Throughout Syd's three-day seminar, I tried every trick I knew to understand what he was saying. He kept talking about how our experience as human beings is based on the Three Principles of Mind, Thought, and Consciousness. Syd explained how using these Three Principles—combined with our free will—determines our experience in life.

He also said every human being on the planet has the same sense of an absolute reality, but it shows up differently for each person. He taught us the following: We are the indeed the authors of our lives.

- Even if we've lived as victims using our gifts to create

---

[7] Sydney Banks. *The Missing Link: Reflections on Philosophy & Spirit*, Lone Pine Publishing, 1998. p. 92.

a fearful, insecure reality, we can also use our gifts to access an inner wisdom that's shared by all.

- We each have access to innate health and wisdom that gets veiled by our thinking.
- Enjoying healthy mental functioning is only one thought away.
- The answers to our issues are straightforward, but we're overlooking them.

All of this made intellectual sense, but I hadn't yet experienced the profound peace others had found through the Three Principles. Whenever Syd fielded a question on a specific issue, such as unhappiness or jealousy, he steered the questioner back to examining these principles. I tried that too, but peace and understanding didn't happen for me.

So I tried relaxing, I tried hard. I tried concentrating. I tried *not* concentrating. I saw that some people were getting it, but others weren't—including me. After three days, I was in the last session and still not understanding. That's when Sydney said, "That's it." For a split second, my mind let down its defenses, and then I, too, got it. *I experienced a fundamental paradigm shift in the way I "saw" the world.* I felt calm and at peace, yet alert and aware. I had a completely new perspective on my thinking.

What he was saying became true for me as the chooser of my thoughts. I felt the incredible power of my free will. It was me who chose to take some thoughts seriously and to discard others. I was an active participant in my life, not a victim of circumstance. I didn't *have* to think as if my life depended on it. I could see it was taking its own course, and the best thing I could do was keep my thinking out of the way. What a relief.

I realize now that for that short, indefinable moment, I had stopped taking my thinking seriously *once I had stopped trying*. The finality of his statement "That's it" caught me unaware. He had stopped and for some reason, I stopped, too.

After coming home from the seminar, I excitedly wanted to share this

"Aha!" moment with everyone I knew. Not surprisingly, I encountered the same polite but noncommittal reception for the Three Principles that I'd first noted in myself.

Workplace Pressures

When a new paradigm comes along, people who *do* understand it don't make a lot of sense to those who *don't*. So, after that seminar, I spent a lot of time with people who had taken the Three Principles to heart. I also met with Syd six times—at his conferences and at his home on Salt Spring Island, British Columbia.

At the time I was still working in multinational corporations, busy in my corporate career, and consumed with this question: *How could I bring this understanding to the workplace where mental pressures on people are immense?* After all, work is where we play out the great psychological drama we call our lives. Because people don't postpone acting out their personal issues until they're at home, the potential for business to benefit from this paradigm shift could be huge.

Being secular and psychological in nature, the Three Principles could provide ways to uncover mindfulness in a business setting. People often perform mindfulness practices—yoga, meditation, contemplation—while away from the workplace. But as soon as they return to work, the benefits of these mindfulness practices evaporate in minutes or hours. At best, they last no longer than a day.

In contrast, understanding the Three Principles allows people to be mindful in *all* situations. It unlocks the secret to resolving business issues that defy easy solutions. For example, they address:

- Why we spend so much time in unproductive meetings.

- Why no one seems to listen to each other.

- How to establish a key sense of connection with others.

Chapter 3: Be Aware of How You THINK

- How to lead with authenticity and integrity.

- Why, collectively, we don't think straight, resolve conflict, reduce stress, and achieve work-life balance.

As I continued working with the Three Principles in business, I understood at a deeper level how business issues *indeed* stem from our thinking.

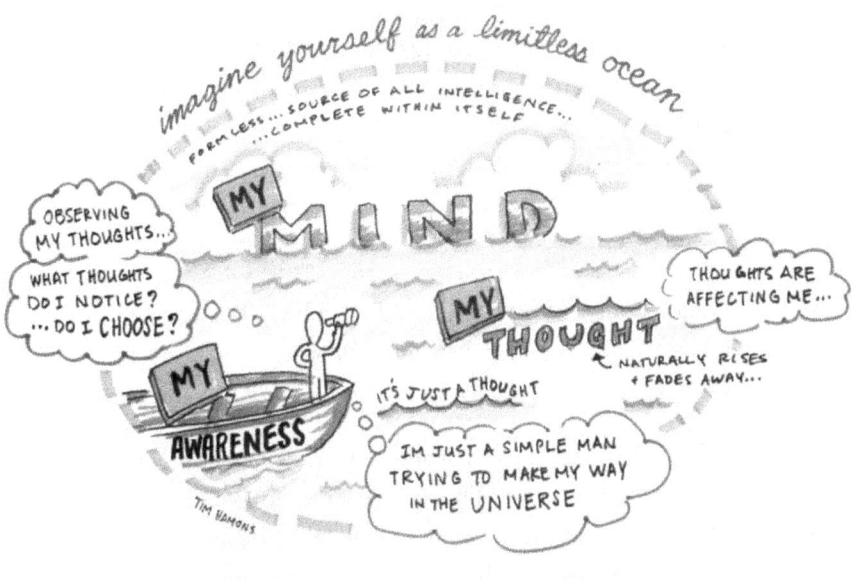

We Create Our Experience of the World with Our Thoughts

With the divine gifts of Mind, Thought, and Consciousness, we paint a picture of the world. It tends to be a grainy, black-and-white, doom-filled affair. When we point out the possibility of living in a glorious technicolor world with Dolby surround sound and fascinating characters, we meet resistance. Even though that response portrays a dull, poorly-defined representation of a far more exciting reality, it is *our* picture. Because we created it, we find it difficult to let go. We think those thoughts we've been collecting all of our lives are in fact our true identity. Sadly, most people would rather die than let go of them.

Yet when we see them for what they are—thoughts that, in our innocence, we decided to take seriously—then a fantastic, beautiful world opens up. We are transformed.

It takes a while to see things differently, particularly concerning things dear to our hearts and minds—that is, our view of the world and our role in it. But the more our world centers on our own thoughts, the more complex is the barrier to true understanding.

What does understanding the Three Principles enable us to do? *Create a mindful space at work in a short time, in an instant, no less.*

Behind the Three Principles is this premise: *You are the author of everything you experience as a human being.* The question then becomes *If you're the author of your experience, why isn't your experience all that good?* Why would you create a not-so-good view of the world? Because you weren't aware you were doing it. Therefore, once you become *aware,* everything changes.

The Three Principles Model

The Three Principles model shows that all of your psychological experience stems from three things: Mind, Thought and Consciousness. These, combined with your free will, create your individual moment-to-moment reality.

Mind

Mind is the world we live in. Our experiences, perceptions, hopes, desires, fears and dreams all occur in mind. We live in a mental world, and it is the only world we can truly know. Mind is infinite, beyond time and space, full and complete. It is the source, without differentiation, of truth, and love, beauty and peace. All of these states are states of things being complete within themselves.

Mind has an energy, of infinite potential, and intelligence, but not yet conceived. Mind is where you truly live. It is where you come home to when you return to yourself, your true nature, that of inner calm and peace. We all share and participate in the same mind.

Thought

Thought is the act of creation, of something seemingly arising out of nothing, yet still comprised of that essential essence. It arises and fades away like a wave crossing the ocean. It is a part of the ocean, and yet simultaneously separate also. Thought is neutral in character. A thought gains its power over us when we notice it and direct our energy toward it. Left alone it will fade away of its own accord.

Consciousness

Consciousness is our soul. We use it to notice some thoughts and ignore others. Our individual experience is determined by which thoughts we notice and what we take seriously. With consciousness we can create a prison with our thoughts, but it is also the key to release us to live as we were truly meant to. What we notice is what we get. We cannot control what thoughts arise, but we can choose which ones to pay attention to.

All Together vs. Separation

The Three Principles operate together in unison. In conjunction with our free will, they are divine gifts that enable us to experience the world. When we pay attention to thoughts of truth and love and beauty we are connected to our true nature, we are home. When we pay attention to isolation, fear, and separation, we create a prison for our souls. The simple beauty of these principles is that, once understood, we can easily return to our spiritual home, at will. We do not need to practice, or exercise, or do anything, we just let go. Understanding the true nature of thought, that it is *just* thought, is the key. We are released from the prison of being a victim of our thinking, and we can regain our birthright to be happy whole and free. When we know it is *just* thought, letting go is easy. When we know our true nature is before thought, we can stop chasing thoughts and sensations to try and achieve inner peace, and just allow it to rise to the surface of our consciousness. When we allow our minds to be quiet and peaceful we free ourselves from the distraction of our thinking; our underlying nature becomes clear. We are peaceful and calm, and we see this is true for others as well. When we communicate at this level, we make a connection—heart to heart, soul to soul.

When we focus on thoughts of separation, of ourselves, we disconnect ourselves from our innate, peaceful, divine nature. We feel frightened and afraid. We put up thought barriers to protect ourselves, yet we are only one thought away from reconnecting with our divine nature.

And where am I in all this?

Chapter 3: Be Aware of How You THINK

We are dominated by a strong sense of self, reinforced from an early age. It seems like an insurmountable barrier. We fear being quiet, of being alone with our thoughts. This sense forms a huge barrier, a defense against the world and a barrier to experiencing our inner peace. This is the world of the ego, the set of thoughts we hold on tightest to, the ones that we think we really are. But the ego is not just a strong self-image, it is actually everything we ever thought about the world. We cannot experience the world without it. It won't go away anytime soon. We cannot live without it; we need it to experience the world. The mistake we make, the fundamental issue that is reinforced from an early age, is that we think it is our true identity. We were told that we should do this and we should do that: be good, study hard, get a good job, please others. All of this is addressing an "I" which is a set of opinions on how the world should be. When the world doesn't conform to this we feel distress. Most advice to relieve this distress is centered on trying even harder to achieve these things. A million motivational speakers are available to reinforce this view. They imply, or even simply state: "You are simply not trying hard enough."

The calm approach is to pause and use our wisdom to discern what is really going on.

Let's try this out:

Get a big piece of paper and:

1. Put a heading at the top: "I will be happy when….."

2. Write down all the things you need to do before you can be truly happy. Use both sides if necessary

3. Ask yourself: "When will now be the time I am happy?"

Take your time

We can deal with our sense of incompleteness in two ways: cover it up with more thinking, such as chasing pleasures and distractions, or we can examine from a calm place what is really going on.

Fear

These fundamental questions can elicit a strong sense of fear. We typically cover this up with distractions rather than deal with it. The truth will set you free, but only if you can get to it. What is this fear? It is the delusion of the separate self, defending itself. It is a delusion because you think you are that collection of thoughts and opinions. It is a case of mistaken identity that has far-reaching consequences. But fear is merely a thought, just like any other thought. This whole mess is just your thinking. If you take it seriously you give it power. All the time your true nature is calling you, that sense of unease and incompleteness is the result of you resisting that call to come home.

Use the gifts of Mind, Thought and Consciousness to listen to that call.

The Trap of Good Thinking and Bad Thinking

When I first came to understand the principles, it unleashed a torrent of insight and connection. These thoughts were beautiful and powerful. It was easy to reject the world of rationality and logic in favor of this world of wonder and completeness. This is a mistake. The world is going on, we cannot avoid it, all types of thought have their place. It is Einstein who said:

"The intuitive mind is a sacred gift and the rational mind is a faithful servant. We have created a society that honors the servant and has forgotten the gift."

When you want to get to the heart of things, use the intuitive mind: talking to people, connecting, problem-solving, strategizing. The intuitive mind is the only way to get there.

Once you are sure of what you want to do, the rational mind is a powerful ally. Just don't put the cart before the horse.

Finding Calm

Here is an important piece of advice to remember. I did this the hard way for it to make sense. I had to work it out for myself. Here is the easy way: *Look for the feeling.*

Your experience as a human being is that of living in the feeling of your thoughts. Your thoughts are the post-experiential rationalization of the initial feeling.

Yes, going back to the intellectual mind will only take you further away from what you seek. More thinking is not the answer. Instead, look inside—look for the *feeling*.

Remember, calm is your innate state before a thought occurs. Your innate state is peaceful but aware. It is open to all possibility, not decided on a particular view. It is the state of being in the now—seeing things as they actually *are*, not how you want them to be. Don't get stuck in the past. The past tends to be about regret. Forgiveness is giving up of all hope of a better past. Forgive yourself and forgive others. You were all doing the best you could with what you knew at the time.

Don't go to the future, of seeing things as you want them to be, that is desire. There is in fact nothing, or no-thing, that will make you sustainably happy, because your innate, happy nature is one free of thought.

Rather, see things simply as they are now: *full of potential, rich and vibrant.*

Our innate nature reveals itself in different forms. In terms of what we experience, it reveals itself as beauty—things being perfect and whole in themselves. In terms of how we think, it reveals itself as insight and wisdom, a glimpse of the underlying truth. In terms of emotion, it reveals itself as love, the sense of completeness and oneness with everything and everyone. In terms of spirituality, it reveals itself as our communion with God. All of these are the result of letting go, not of creating.

So, going forward, don't look for the *thought*. Instead, look for the *feeling*, that feeling of calm.

CHAPTER 4
Let It Go

Any intelligent fool can make things bigger, more complex, and more violent. It takes a touch of genius —and a lot of courage— to move in the opposite direction.

— Albert Einstein

Have you ever received a comment on your report card similar to the one I always got: "If only Mark could focus more, his results would be better." Well, I have news for you. The key to success is actually to focus *less*, not *more*.

Focus is the enemy of insight. Throughout our lives it's been reinforced again and again that the key to solving problems is to think more. We've been told our problem is that we don't concentrate enough. If only we could cut out all of those distractions and direct our thoughts to the matter in hand, things would be better. When we try that, we end up in a state with our minds *full*. With the clutter of all those thoughts, there is no room for clarity or insight.

This leads to an important aspect of Practical Mindfulness, the third great secret: *To think better, you need to let go of whatever is on your mind.*

"Let It Go"—the key to mindful action—maybe almost as extreme a cliché as Nike's motto "JUST DO IT." However, you can't *think* your way to a better thought or a better mindset. Nor can you cover up any underlying turmoil for long. You just have to truly *let go* and let your innate wisdom shine through.

This can be an unnerving prospect. It is not so much learning how to do something new as it is unlearning something that has been reinforced over and over again in the past. Your natural state is one of insight and connection. To be authentic you don't have to learn anything. This is your natural state. You just have to let go of the thinking that is in the way. Similarly, to listen to someone, to make a connection, you don't have to learn new skills. This is our natural talent. We all have it. It's just that we cover it up in varying degrees of effectiveness. This may explain something that has been bothering you: we all have our moments of being 'on song', 'in the moment', 'in flow'. We struggle to be able to do so at will. This is because we think these moments are the result of effort. The truth is they are the result of us letting go.

Similarly, we all have experienced the 'high' of achieving something. It is a powerful feeling. It is tempting to try and re-create it, by setting up more and more things to achieve. The truth is the 'high' is generated by our allowing ourselves to relax for a moment once we believe we have reached our goal, or possess something we desire. We allow our true nature to shine through for some time, until our thinking starts up again and we demand more before we can allow ourselves to be satisfied again.

This 'letting go' is a natural ability we all have. Have you seen a toddler throwing a tantrum in a supermarket and how people try to help by distracting the child? Once the child is distracted, the disturbing thought is forgotten. Likewise, distraction is the key that may help *you* drop your disturbing thoughts. This natural ability to drop thought has been in abeyance so long, people have forgotten they have it. But it's time to rediscover this ability.

When I ask my clients under what circumstances insights appear, they often say "anywhere but at work", and certainly when they're not thinking about work at all. Insight, then, seems to be a rare occurrence. Clearly this requires creating space in our heads so our innate wisdom can shine through. We have to let something go.

Like 'JUST DO IT', the command 'Let It Go' is great advice, but easier said than done. Even worse, once we start thinking, our minds start filling up again. But there's one surefire way to let your thoughts go so insight can shine in: *Get LISTENED to.*

Sometimes Nothing Needs to be Said: A True Story

Soon after I first understood the Three Principles, I developed a reputation as a trouble-shooter and project turnaround specialist. My approach was simple: I listened to what people had to say. They normally knew what was wrong and what to fix, but they didn't have enough time and mental space to actually do it.

One memorable situation sticks in my mind. I was told to report to the head office of a major insurance company to meet the CIO. A project was in trouble. I had caught an early morning flight, taken a taxi to the office in the CBD (Central Business District), and met my contacts. They seemed nervous about the situation I would soon walk into—a 9 a.m. meeting in the CIO's office—with miniscule understanding of the problem.

The initial signs were *not* promising. The contacts escorted me to the top floor, took me to the office, and then they stood diffidently outside. I overheard the CIO talking angrily on the phone, and I sensed something else wasn't right. He gestured to me to sit down, so I did. Then he continued with the call in an angry and agitated manner for the next 10 minutes without further acknowledging my presence.

"This will be interesting," I thought.

In this situation, I could do nothing except sit and wait. He finally put down the phone and rose slowly to his feet, clutching his back. Without looking at me even then, he said, "My back is killing me. I'm going in for an operation on Friday, and I'm just holding out until then."

I nodded, even though he wasn't looking at me. Clearly, he was in immense physical pain.

For five minutes, he walked slowly around the room talking to himself. I just sat there, neutral. Then he suddenly came over to the low table in front of where I sat, grabbed a piece of paper, and started drawing a diagram.

"The trouble as I see it is this," he said.

He then drew up a diagram showing the stakeholders, indicating who was a supporter and who wasn't. He circled one and said, "The problem is, this guy is the customer, but he's not owning the result. He's just sitting back and sniping. It's politics. He's got to have skin in the game, and he has to contribute some resources so we get his requirements clear. His department has to show ownership. I'll talk to the CEO about it. That's the only way it's going to happen.

"Now," he continued, "Christine, the project manager. She's done herself no favors. I've supported her, and technically she's done a great job. She knows how to fix the requirements and get the design right. But she has annoyed too many people with her dogmatic approach. She may have been right, but it's not the way things are done here. I'll have to move her off. I'll find her another position."

Then he turned to me directly and said, "Thank you. Thank you for being such a help. I'm really grateful I can go and have my operation knowing we can sort this out. I know you'll have to do a report, so I want you to stay here for the next two weeks to get the details clarified. I'll get the actions underway. Go and work with the team to get everyone on the right track. I'm so pleased to clear this up."

With this, he shook my hand and showed me the door.

I swear, in the entire meeting, I'd not said a word.

When we're truly listened to, without interruption, our current thinking somehow dissipates, and fresh, deeper thinking appears. The longer we're truly listened to, the closer we get to the innate wisdom that lives at our core.

Of course, to be listened to can be a rare occurrence, but great coaches know this is the key to success. The best coaches have learned the more they take themselves out of the situation, the better the results. They trust their clients are the *only ones* who can identify their issues and the *only ones* who can solve them. Indeed, they know their clients can have ready access to their innate wisdom to do this by simply being calm themselves.

Great *leaders* know this, too. However, in any business organization, there's not usually a lot of listening going on—especially from the leadership.

The Best Teacher or Manager

I often ask people to consider an influential teacher or manager they worked for and describe what the experience was like. Their responses invariably center on the same theme: "The atmosphere was one of trust and confidence. I didn't have to be on my guard. I felt I could say what was on my mind and that person wouldn't judge me."

We explored what actually happened in an example encounter.

"Well, when I went in, I was warmly greeted. Then he devoted all of his attention to me."

Who did the talking?

"Well, I did. He didn't say much at all. I just talked things through and worked things out in front of him. Come to think of it, I'm not sure he said much at all, maybe just a gentle inquiry. I had the feeling he was guiding me somewhere, but he trusted me to find the answer."

How did you perform in that job or class?

"Well, it was my best subject. I got great marks, but it seemed really easy. We all got great marks."

A study run in the U.S. attempted to discover the characteristics of a great teacher. The methodology was a bit unusual. Those conducting the study asked around the school to identify who the best teachers were. As with management, a study can produce all sorts of criteria, but usually the star performers are obvious. They have a sense of calm and an air of confidence.

The researchers studied the teachers for a number of months, trying to ascertain what factors made a difference. It wasn't the structure of the teaching, the curriculum, or even the teachers' style. It was one thing that happened commonly among these star teachers: They all spent time every day with each individual pupil.

Can you guess how long they spent on average?

Thirty seconds.

Can you imagine what the interaction was like?

Nothing spectacular. Just a clear interest in what the pupil was doing.

Have you got 30 seconds in your day for each of your employees?

It's More than Important; Listening is Crucial

For some reason that I don't fully understand, being listened to helps us access our inner wisdom. It seems that talking things through is how we air our useless thoughts, allowing them to dissipate in the light of awareness allowing us access to a deeper level of insight.

Yet listening isn't a strong suit for most people in business. They seem to think they don't have time to listen, that events are so urgent they have to state actions forcefully.

You can find lots of advice on how to listen better because doing it well is regarded as an important skill. From my point of view, it's more than important—it's *crucial*. Incidentally, most techniques are designed to help you listen better when you *don't want to* listen. Our instruction focusses on *why* listening is the single most important thing we can do.

Typically in a conversation, we comment on the first thing people say. We're then stuck at that initial level of thinking. The problem is, the first thing that comes out of people's mouths normally isn't that insightful. We might even feel a need to correct it. Because we don't trust that they can access their own wisdom and insight, we want to give them a helping hand.

Resist that urge.

What happens if we allow people to speak a bit longer? Their level of thinking rises automatically, provided we don't interrupt. This is a bit unnerving at first. If you do interrupt, the effect is lost. Just let the person go on a little more than you are used to. Don't comment, just let them talk. A little more time at this stage saves a lot of time later on.

But, typically, we don't allow people to speak. Instead, we offer an opinion. We're thinking about our own view and looking for an opening so we can talk too, which means we're *not* listening carefully. The person we're talking to can sense this.

We may think that relating something from our experience may be helpful. Nine times out of ten it is not. What is important is our client's experience. not ours. Only they can solve their own issues.

We know when we're not being listened to. It happens all the time. It's the typical modus operandi of business: everyone struggling to be heard, talking more and more to try and make people listen, with building frustration

>The CALM approach looks like this:

Listen.

Don't think about what you're going to say next.

Listen.

Don't be put off by the first thing the person says. It's usually not cogent or meaningful. Rather, listen for the person's innate wisdom. If you say anything, it might be, "Tell me more." That's about it.

You'll be astonished.

Question: What stops you from truly listening to someone?

Practical Mindfulness Exercise

The next time you're in a position to listen to someone, rather than thinking ahead about your response, say in an interested voice, "Tell me more."

Repeat.

CHAPTER 5
Getting in the MOOD

If you're not in the mood, you can't do that stuff right.

– J.D. Salinger, *The Catcher in the Rye*

Solve the Problem

One of my favorite movies is *Disclosure*, starring Michael Douglas and Demi Moore. Set in a fictional Seattle technology company called DigiCOM, it tells about office intrigue, company politics, and sexual harassment. From my view, it's an accurate depiction of the technology industry. One of its motifs is an email sent to the male protagonist that states only this: "Solve the problem." This spurs him each time to look more deeply into what's going on behind office distractions. He receives this message a number of times until he does, indeed, uncover the real problem.

I think about this motif often when consulting with client organizations. What's the underlying problem the leaders need to solve—the core issue? They receive advice from any number of organizations, but in many cases they don't fully accept the solutions, because these solutions simply don't feel right. That is their innate wisdom at work, telling them the truth: they haven't solved the problem. They go on management retreats, employ mindfulness approaches, and dig deep into their souls—all with a sense of general dissatisfaction. Nothing hits the spot.

So, exactly what's the problem they need to solve? It is this:

The people in their organization are more or less in a permanent bad mood.

What got them there?

Did the leadership have anything to do with it?

If you were to do just one thing to boost your performance and that of the organization, it's this: *Pay attention to and address your own mood.*

Measurements

A huge industry has sprung up focusing on the "climate" of organizations—measuring, incentivizing, and offering advice on how to improve the climate, the organizational mood. Managers become measured on their performance as coach and cheerleader rather than director of a series of tasks.

The evidence is compelling, as several resources cite:

- "Roughly 50 to 75 percent of how employees perceive their organization's climate can be traced to the actions of one person: the leader."[8]

- "Moods influence how effectively people work; upbeat moods boost cooperation, fairness, and business performance...."[9]

- "In a study of 19 insurance companies, the climate

---

8   C. Kelner, S. Rivers, and K. O'Connell. *Managerial Style as a Behavioral Predictor of Organizational Climate*, McBer & Company, Boston, 1996.

9   S. Barsade and M. Gibson. "Group Emotion: A View From the Top and Bottom" in *Research on Managing Groups and Teams*, eds. D. Gruenfeld et al., JAI Press, Greenwich, CT, 1998.

created by the CEOs among their direct reports predicted the business performance of the entire organization: In 75 percent of cases, climate alone accurately sorted companies into high versus low profits and growth."[10]

- "A study of 62 CEOs and their top teams from Fortune 500 companies found that the more positive the overall moods of the people in the top management team, the more cooperatively they worked together—and the better the company's business results. . . . [T]he longer a company was run by a management team that did not get along, the poorer that company's market return."[11]

Our fourth great secret states: *It's not your thinking that's the key to success; it's your mood.*

Mood Mapper™

Why is this so? Let's do an exercise using the Mood Mapper. This exercise allows you and your organization to understand the powerful effect of your state of mind (or sum of your thinking) on your collective performance. Once again, the basic idea was developed by Alexander Caillet of the Accompli Group, and he's happy to allow me to use it here. I believe the more people get the hang of this powerful tool, the better place the world will be.

Following is a Mood Mapper form, either photocopy this, or even better, go to www.thecalmrevolution.com and download a beautiful full-color version.

---

10   D. Williams. *Leadership for the 21st Century: Life Insurance Leadership Study*, LOMA/Hay Group, Boston, 1995.

11   S. Barsade, A. Ward, et al. "To Your Heart's Content: A Mode of Affective Diversity in Top Management Teams," *Administrative Science Quarterly* 45, 2000: 802-836.

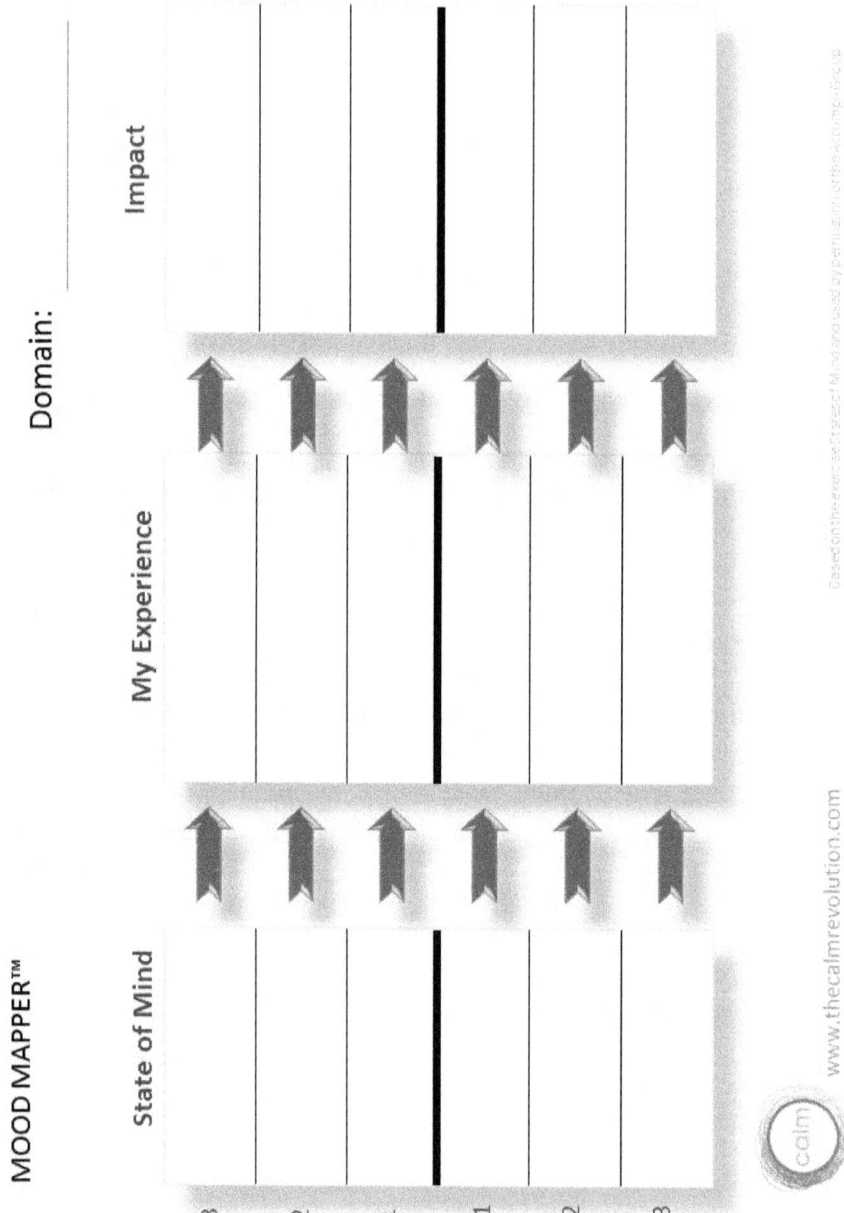

Here are your instructions:

1. Each row corresponds to a level of state of mind. Three rows are situated above a dark solid line, which we call the 'neutral line'. These three rows are labeled +1, +2, and +3 and correspond to states of mind that are 'above the line' or higher in nature. Three other rows are situated below the neutral line. These three rows are labeled -1, -2, and -3 and correspond to states of mind that are 'below the line' or lower in nature.

2. Beginning with the bottom row, ask the following question: "What words or phrases would you use to describe a -3 state of mind?" Write them in the box. Choose three words or phrases.

3. Repeat the question for each one of the other five rows, moving sequentially up from -3 to +3, and record your responses.

4. Select one domain of study that interests you and write the domain on the blank line at the top right of the page. Possible domains include: Time, Money, Parenting, Relationships, Listening, Managing Conflict, Perspective, Committing, Accountability, Collaboration, Teamwork, Decision-making, Managing Change, Productivity, Performance.

5. Using the rows in the middle column of the form, answer the following question for each state-of-mind level: "What is my experience of this domain when I am in this state of mind?" For example, if the word selected for the -2 level is "frustrated" and the domain is 'Parenting', the question becomes: "What is my experience of parenting when I am in a frustrated state of mind?" Write your answer in the cell.

6. Using the rows in the final column of the form, ask

this: "What is my impact on others when I'm in this state of mind?" For example, say the word for the -2 level is *frustrated*, the domain is Parenting, and your experience of parenting in this frame of mind is that it's time-consuming, a burden, and a chore. Now consider how your children respond to you when you're in this mood. The answer probably won't be pretty.

Be sure to sit back and reflect on your answers. They're highly revealing.

This exercise has been conducted thousands of times within various organizations. Following are examples of responses in the domains of Decision Making and Performance.

Chapter 5: Getting In The MOOD 79

MOOD MAPPER™

Domain: Decision Making

State of Mind	My Experience	Impact
Elated	Engaged, Pushing for a decision, Deciding too quickly	Over ambitious decisions, chasing many initiatives that don't come to fruition
Energized	Focused, Researched, Collaborative, Assured, Well thought through decisions	Decisive, innovative approaches that are implemented with a passion
Clear	Balanced and Measured, Patient, Participative	Steady Progress, Sensible
Tired	Letting someone else drive the process, Impatient, Over reliance on advisers.	Unsteady Progress, Activity without real insight. Go through the motions
Worried	Disempowering, short-sighted decisions to relieve immediate pain	More problems occur, subversive, passive aggressive. Looking for a hero
Depressed	Inability to make any decision, Avoidance, Emotional reactions	Abdication of responsibility and power

www.thecalmrevolution.com

Based on the exercise States of Mind and used by permission of the Arcomph Group

MOOD MAPPER™　　　　Domain: *Performance*

State of Mind	My Experience	Impact
Fulfilled	Persistence, High Resilience, Generosity	Breakthrough performance
Happy	Engaged, Synchronized, able to take on more	Effective and Efficient
Satisfied	Smooth, focused, steady, engaged	Productive
Disengaged	50/50, Inconsistent, distracted, lower energy	Uneven performance. Go through the motions, don't take on anything new
Frustrated	Procrastination, Avoidance	Broken commitments or no commitments, Start and stop behaviors
Exhausted	Blaming, Justifying, Inability to engage	Negative results

Based on the expert seStates of Mind and used by permission of the Accompli Group

www.thecalmrevolution.com

Our first example takes place in the decision-making environment. Does this look like any place you know? It's interesting to note that having high energy and excitement levels is not necessarily a good thing for great decision making.

The second mood map brings out interesting points. Normally, when the energy in an organization flags, the chosen remedy is to energize it, or raise it. Often this job is outsourced to a motivational speaker. With an external stimulus, the company can experience a short-term gain. However, people and organizations rapidly fall back to their normal level because of their habitual thinking and mood.

In the 'Performance' domain, when people are asked to name the highest level of mood, the answer is 'Fulfilled', not 'Energized'. To get people to feel fulfilled, a lot of needs must be met. In particular, they must be encouraged and allowed to perform to their potential. That's a tough assignment, particularly when we look at its counterpart below the line: Disengaged. Lack of energy is not the problem; keeping that energy focused *in the right place* becomes the goal.

I love this exercise because it always generates powerful insights, and each time we run it, we uncover something new.

It's interesting to see that being calm is great, but more progress is made when we're a bit more energized. However, being *too* energized and passionate can have negative effects. In all of this, the intention is to be mindful of your thinking: *It needs to change to respond to what is in front of you.* There is no one-size-fits-all. Sometimes, but not often, it's even good to be angry!

Note the bold-colored line at the zero level. There's a fundamental difference in how we experience the world depending on whether our state of mind is above or below this line. The participants on our courses have said these things:

- "Below the line, it's all about *me*, and above the line, it's all about *we*."

- "It's a waste of time doing any planning until we get ourselves above the line, otherwise our plans will reflect our thinking at that level: defensive, conservative, unclear."

- "You can't think your way out of a bad mood; that's what got you there in the first place."

- "Above the line, it's ecocentric; we are thinking about the impact on everything. Below the line, it's egocentric; people thinking about the impact on themselves."

What are your insights?

Noticing Our Thoughts

Our experience changes from moment to moment depending on what thoughts we're noticing. *These thoughts create our mood.*

Some people experience wild mood swings; some stay at about the same level. When we notice our personal, fearful thoughts through the use of consciousness, the world seems to be a threatening place. We respond accordingly, putting up defenses and closing up shop. When we notice our true, innate nature through the use of consciousness, our sense of time evaporates. What's the evidence? We're truly in the moment, actions seem effortless, and the results spectacular.

And here's the good news: You can use the CALM approach to achieve that great mood. Remember the four secrets:

1. Understand the CAUSE of your thinking.

2. Be AWARE of how your thinking works.

3. LET GO of unhelpful thinking by LISTENING to each other.

4. Find that great MOOD.

Look for the Mood Mapper in later chapters to address specific business issues such as meetings, stress, and effective execution. In the meantime, let's examine another fascinating use of the Mood Mapper, this time as a diagnostic tool.

What's My Organization's Culture?

Most of our clients have a big issue with culture. The organization may have conducted an engagement or a cultural climate survey to measure how engaged their employees have been with their work. The results are usually disappointing, so the clarion call goes out: "We need to fix this!"

But how? First of all, we seek to understand the root cause of the issue, so we apply the Mood Mapper tool on the management team.

84 Calm: The Key to Clarity, Connectedness, and Presence at Work

MOOD MAPPER™

Domain: Management Team Mindset

State of Mind	Staff Experience	Impact
Ecstatic, Elated, Euphoric	Consultative, Clear, Communication of Vision	Inspired; Go above and beyond
Happy, Excited, Confident	Trusting, Share the Vision, Motivating	Catch the good mood, confident, innovative
Good, Businesslike, Active	Clear Direction, Focus on what's important. Light Touch	Responsive, Take Initiative, Energetic
Neutral, Coping, Hands On	Stick to Routine, Process Orientated, Hands on	Only do the necessary. No oomph!
Desperate, Anxious, Worried	Suspicious, Focus on Control, Management do everything themselves, proscriptive	Resentful, Passive Aggressive
Hopeless, Depressed	Paralyzed, Angry	Leaving or Left

Based on the exercise States of Mind and used by permission of the Accompli Group

www.thecalmrevolution.com

Now, if you want to know what the real management mindset is, look at the behavior you observe on the right and then look along the row to the left. This is normally met with disbelief. How can we be in the negative mindset? The truth is, what you *think* you are doing and what you are *actually* doing are two different things.

Yet people react to how we act, not what we think. For example, those on most management teams believe they are open to new suggestions from their staff, but when presented with new proposals, they typically respond with critical questioning, nit-picking, and caution. The way most management teams *think* they act and how they actually *act* are quite different. It's a matter of self-awareness. Normally, the management mindset in most companies isn't good news. So what's the solution?

The Shadow of Leadership

One of the most influential pieces of research ever conducted regarding management behavior raised the concept of "The Shadow of the Leader," developed by Larry Senn of the Senn-Delaney Group.[12] He discovered that the actions and behaviors of an organization directly mirror those of its leadership. That refers to the leader's actions and behaviors, mind you, not what they *say*.

Leaders shape their cultures through a powerful combination of *message aligned with action*. Through actions, attitudes, and messages, they cast a shadow that influences everyone around them. That shadow may be strong and inspiring, or it may be weak and dispiriting, but it always exists. It's a reflection of everything the leader says and does.

Leaders lead without knowing it. Actions speak loudly. And someone is always watching.

Too Much Communication

Traditionally, the answer to improving culture has been to communicate

---

12   www.senndelaney.com/spotlight_jan09_larrysenn.html

more, but you need to be careful to *not* communicate more of the wrong thing.

When leaders ask, "What is wrong with my people?" we have to delicately steer them to the real question, "What impact are your actions having on your team?" We then take them through the impact their state of mind has on others and help them see the contribution *they* are making to the situation.

Leaders are used to modifying their actions at the behavioral level. They try hard to show the right attributes, which is always a struggle. However, when they understand the power of the Three Principles, they then see the key is the *awareness of their thinking*.

What Can You Do?

So if you're a leader, what can you do? As Gandhi famously said, "Be the change you want to see in the world." In this case, rather than worry about your staff, *work on yourself*.

George Pransky is one of the leading psychologists who worked with Sydney Banks in the early days and throughout his life. He described the effect of our individual state of mind on the others around us as follows[13]:

If I am in a state of angry indignation . . .	. . . others will fight me tooth and nail.
If I am in a state of annoyance and irritation . .	. . . others will drag their feet.
If I am in a state of contentment . . .	. . . others will join me.
If I am in a state of appreciation . . .	. . . others will put themselves out for me.
If I am in a state of deep gratitude . . .	. . . others will pull out all the stops to help.

---

13   George Pransky, The Relationship Handbook. Pransky and Associates; 2nd Ed. 2013. p. 83.

What Gandhi said is true: First you change yourself, then the world will change around you.

Let's look at another actual case. An organization had found itself bouncing between two different states. The first was a passive-aggressive resistance movement, a legacy of the previous management team dominated by an autocratic CEO. The second was an unfocused, exhausting stream of new ideas and initiatives driven by the new CEO. He was brought in by the board as an attempted antidote. Both approaches have their drawbacks, as indicated in the following Mood Mapper. You'll see two things going on at the same time:

1. A neutral state of mind, a form of defense mechanism. The attitude of the senior managers was only to cope, not to try and do anything exceptional. They felt ambivalent. Things were "just okay." Their own attitude toward change was uncertain. They described this as Humpty Dumpty sitting on the wall waiting for someone to try something else—and fail. Why? Because they themselves worked for a chief executive who was autocratic in style. They had tried to do the right thing but, in the end, realized all power lay with the chief executive. Therefore, as they concluded, "Why go out of our way to do something, just to be slapped down or undermined?" The effect on their staff was even more dramatic. Rather than fearing change, the issue for most of the staff was that the organization wouldn't fix what needed fixing. Their attempts to do anything were stymied. In this case, the action (or inaction) of the management team breeds three things: an attitude of frustration, a re-litigation of previous decisions, and an absence of decision making.

2. A euphoric, enthusiastic state of mind from a new leader. This results in an organization that's exhausted from *too much* change. While it felt exciting to be in the presence of an inspiring leader, people

State of Mind	Sense of Time	Attitude to Change	Leadership Behaviours	Organisation Impact
Excited; Euphoric; Enthusiastic	Don't Notice Time	??????	Unreal expectations; Exciting; Too Many Ideas; Non-stop; Sugar High; Hysteria; Hyperactive; Risk of Burn Out	Confusion; Frustration; Exhaustion; Frustration; Constant Change; Shiny Object Syndrome; Burn Out; Fear; Unpredictable; Everything is a Blur
Happy; Light Hearted; Joyful	Time is enough; Able to do a little more with the time we have	Bring it on; Opportunities; Enthusiastic	Collaborative; Production; Respectful; Innovative; Unified; United; Leadership; Constructively Challenge ; Forward Thinking	Enthusiasm; Awareness; Change; Growth; Development; Engagement; Healthy Debate; Safe; Positive; Learning Environment
Content; Satisfied; Comfortable	Time is adequate; Manageable; I am in control	Give it a go; Go along with it; "What's in it for me?"	Do it as it's always done; Teamwork; Predictable; Group Think; Safe; Positive; Management	Status Quo; Safe; Comfortable; Why Change?; Routine; "She'll be Right"; Complacent; Not Progressive; Frustration
Neutral; Care less; OK; Ambivalent	Everything seems sluggish and slow	"Prove it to me"; Humpty Dumpty sat on the wall...	Indecision; Complacent; Not Focused; Go with the Flow; Slow; "Not Worth the Fight"; Inefficient	Frustration; Re-litigation; No/Slow Decisions; Apathy; Living in the Now; Bored; Unproductive
Unhappy; Grumpy; miserable	Time drags / stands still ; there never seems enough	Resistant; Blocking; Passive Aggressive behaviours	Rudeness; Mistrust and Distrust; Not Present; Dictatorial; Silo; Self Interest; Individual; Confrontational	Confusion; Anarchy; Negotiate/Play Off; Reactive; Rudeness; Mistrust and Distrust; Disconnected; Confrontational
Desperate; Despair; Depressed	Time is a never ending burden; it is endless and long and drawn out	Adversarial; Aggressive; "Henny Penny"	Isolation; Despair; Ignoring; Disengaged; Absent	Chaos; Check Out; Disengaged; Everything is Pointless; No Focus; No Direction

experienced a set of unreal expectations and non-stop idea generation that resembled a sugar high. The impact? Confusion, exhaustion, and frustration with the constant change. Some call it "the shiny object syndrome" with the attention always being directed to the next new thing. This got in the way of the organization's operational effectiveness with many essential tasks remaining undone.

3. Falling in the middle is the most desired attitude: A happy, light-hearted joyful mood. This would lead to an organization whose people would be open and enthusiastic about doing new things, yet grounded in a positive reality. The leaders would demonstrate appropriate behaviors; they'd be collaborative, respectful, innovative, and unified. Their challenges would be constructive, not obstructive. To create this kind of environment that everyone wanted could actually be easy: simply keep the mood light.

The organization was experiencing both the shadow of the present leader and an echo of the leadership that has been in place before. It's common for this echo to be highly persistent. In our experience, it takes at least 18 months for the shadow of a new regime to take effect. You may wonder why people continue to fight old battles rather than concentrate on the now. Because it simply takes time for things to sink in.

Market Forces

This chart shows another example of how mood can affect actions and results. It was developed with an audience of budding entrepreneurs.

The implication is clear. Companies that focus on control and compliance—and therefore "dumb down" the natural creative spirit of their employees—can succeed in their current market conditions. However, they're extremely vulnerable when market conditions change.

MOOD	ACTIONS	IMPACT
ECSTATIC ELATED EUPHORIC	DECISIVE CLEAR	DEFINING THE MARKET TAKE OVER COMPETITORS
HAPPY EXCITED CONFIDENT	EXPANSIVE SEE OPPORTUNITIES EVERYWHERE SEE RISK AS POSITIVE	MAKING YOUR OWN MARKET NICHE OUTMANOEUVRE COMPETITORS
RELIEF ENCOURAGED HOPEFUL	RESPONSIVE TAKE INITIATIVE ENERGETIC	SUCCESSFUL IN CURRENT MARKET COMPETING STRONGLY
SO-SO NUMB NEUTRAL	SAME OLD ROUTINE BUSY BUT NOT EFFECTIVE	WILL BE OVERTAKEN BY EVENTS AND MORE AGILE COMPETITORS
DESPERATE ANXIOUS WORRIED	GO THROUGH THE MOTIONS ASK FOR HELP TRY EVERYTHING	ONLY A MATTER OF TIME BEFORE FAILURE
HOPELESS DEPRESSED SUICIDAL	NOTHING PARALYSED	BUSINESS CLOSURE

Remember the principles of CALM:

- The root *cause* of all of this is your thinking.

- Be *aware* it's your thinking, and you can change it at any time.

- Change your thinking by *letting go* of what you're holding on to.

- Your *mood* will naturally lift.

PART II:

APPLICATIONS

1. Stress and Resilience
2. Busyness
3. Planning
4. Clarity
5. Meetings
6. Procrastination

CHAPTER 6
Less Stress, More Success

Life is a contact sport.

- Sydney Banks

Is there such a thing as good stress? Not unless you can take heed of it as a warning signal that things are not well. In this chapter we'll look at how we can use CALM to address a problem that is prevalent in our business lives: the mental and physical toll of stress.

In another challenging project I led, our customer had made fundamental decisions that were destined to cause problems. We'd done our best to warn the customer's people, but seemingly it had become a matter of pride for them to stick to their guns and see it through, rather than admit they had made a bad choice. This is common in business: substituting extreme effort for clear thinking.

The pressure gnawed at me and kept me up at night. I did *not* want to go through this one more time. In the morning, I drove into work for an early start and went right past the car park entrance. I simply couldn't physically make the turn to go to work. So I drove around the block and tried again. Again, I just couldn't turn the wheel, enter the car park, and get down to business. Like an airplane that can't land, chalk up two missed approaches. So I drove down to the harbor, looked out over the water, and mused.

I remembered what I'd been told about stress from the practitioners of the Three Principles. Mentally and physically, stress was dangerous, even crippling—something I knew from observing my colleagues. In this situation, my body had decided not to let me go to work. Enough was enough.

I also remembered the three-step plan to use in emergencies. It starts with asking these questions:

1. Can you change the situation?

    No, I thought. I had tried my best.

2. Can you change your thinking about the situation?

    No. I had tried everything I knew.

3. Then it's time to remove yourself from the situation.

Later in the morning, I did manage to make it into work. By then, I'd decided to tell my manager I wanted off the project.

"You know what that means" he stated more than asked.

"The end of my career here." We both knew it.

I left with a happy heart because I'd finally listened to my innate wisdom. With this departure, I had given myself the gift of time to develop and share the CALM approach—and the rest is history.

Less Stress, More Success

One problem dominates the business world—that is, people are too busy to think straight. It's an accepted belief that stress is an inevitable part of the work environment and can be beneficial. Unfortunately, that belief only aggravates the situation.

Being busy is considered a good thing—a sign that you're a great employee—and few employees are measured on results to find out whether that busyness pays off. In fact, in many cases, busyness can seriously impede productivity and creativity.

Most managers figure if they don't put people under pressure, nothing will get done. They've experienced the reward of putting teams under intense pressure for a short time and achieving a result. They're also aware that when they put people under too much pressure, they crack. So they're always experimenting to find that optimal level of stress—not too little, not too much.

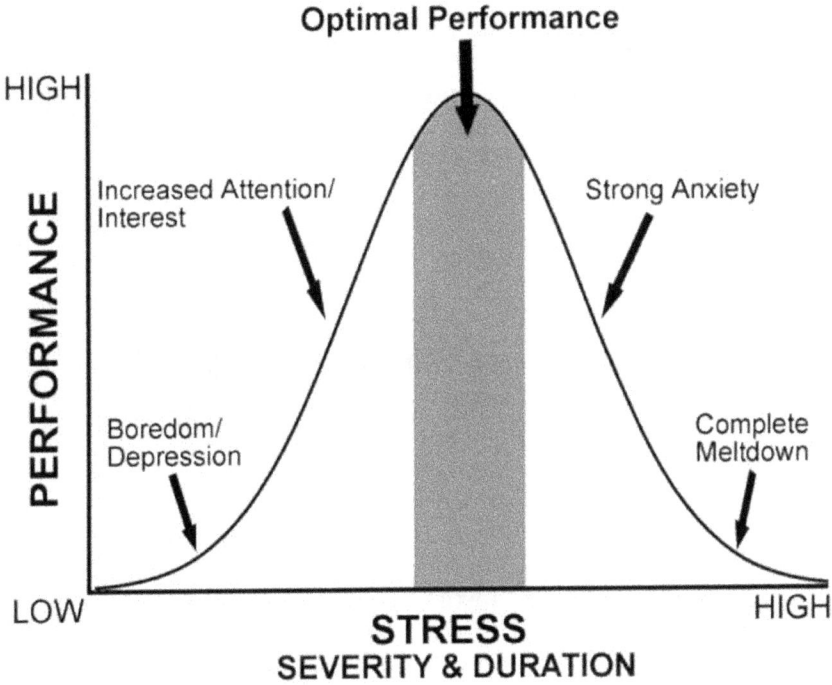

The classic bell curve above illustrates this point: many organisations are habitually on the right hand side of the curve, coping just enough to avoid a complete meltdown, but with disastrous effects on performance.

Considered to be the godfather of stress research, Hans Selye was the first to define stress in a psychological context. He took care to distinguish between a stressor, which was an external event, and the feeling of stress, which was an internal reaction. With even a basic understanding of the Three Principles, it's clear every person will react differently to the same set of stressors in the business world and outside of it. Some people thrive on being pressured to a significant degree, while others become debilitated by stress when pressured even a little.

A key application is for people to understand the true nature and implications of stress. We ask them to compare what they felt and how they acted *when they were stressed* with how they felt and acted *when they were in a secure state of mind*. Here are some common responses:

Stressed State of Mind

- My busy mind blocks my ability to listen to others and to my own common sense.
- I create low self-esteem by repeating negative thoughts from the past.
- I stress myself out by worrying, thinking negative thoughts, going over details, and overthinking.
- I analyze a lot to figure things out, focusing on what is wrong and negative.
- I see 'problems' and 'difficult' situations.
- I easily misinterpret and make incorrect assumptions.
- I make mistakes; I work harder, not smarter.
- I feel rushed and pressured. I treat others badly and don't take care of myself.
- I become unable to effectively manage my time and attention in all important areas of my life (work/life balance).

Natural, Secure State of Mind (Unstressed)

- My thoughts are quiet and focused in the moment.
- I access natural, positive feelings: I am in a 'Good Mood.'
- I experience innate self-esteem and take better care

of myself.

- I access my deeper intelligence: I think wisely and productively.

- I see life with greater perspective and clarity.

- I become more confident: Things work out.

- I listen more deeply to my intuition/common sense and follow this deeper intelligence to get results.

- I experience greater job satisfaction and better productivity.

- I have compassion and a deeper understanding for colleagues and clients.

- I have enough time and energy; I can prioritize easily.

From those responses, it's difficult to believe any benefit at all derives from being stressed. People under stress tend to take a short-term viewpoint, their wider appreciation of the situation deteriorates, and they shrink into self-preservation mode. People who aren't stressed can see the wider picture, take a long-term view, and are more responsive to serving a greater purpose than defending themselves. Therefore, managers in organizations would benefit from *removing* stress from their teams, not *applying* it.

Good Stress and Bad Stress

Is there such a thing as good stress? When Hans Selye first put forward his concepts of stress he distinguished between two responses to a stressor: stimulation, which he called eustress (good stress), and a negative response, which he called distress (bad stress). Neurological research indicates two types of physiological responses to a stressor: a short-term response lasting for about 20 seconds with no longer-term impact, and longer-term impact raising cortisol levels in the body and carrying significant health risks if not addressed. This is the stress we are talking about: if the response to a stressor is exhilaration or excitement or motivation then that is a great thing, but is not the stress we are talking about here. People do not suffer from eustress. However, they certainly suffer from distress.

You may be thinking, "But I need a certain amount of stress to make me get out of bed in the morning."

Really? You've had a great night's sleep and your mind is at rest, but you want to hide in your bed in the morning until you've summoned enough mental strength to face the day? Does feeling stressed get you out of bed—or make you want to stay there?

Practical Mindfulness Exercise

Question: Which organization has invested the most time and money and published the most research on the effect of stress on performance?

Answer: The U.S. military

Question: What did the researchers conclude?

Answer: People perform worse when they're under stress.

Yes, the military deliberately attempts to put their opponents under stress so they perform badly. And in training, they put their own people under stress so they know how to deal with it when someone is shooting at them.

Ironically, most managers put their teams under stress in the mistaken belief that it will improve their performance. Quite the opposite is true: It's the managers' job to minimize stress for those they manage.

Do you habitually put your organization under stress when seeking to improve results? What kind of thinking does this foster? What can *you* do to reduce the stress in your organization?

Resilience and a Hot Air Balloon

Sydney Banks took great pains to point out that humans have an inherent mental healing process. In the same way a *physical* healing process naturally kicks in when we incur a physical injury, a *mental* healing process goes to work when our mental health suffers.

For example, he said, imagine you've broken your arm. Each time you visited the doctor, would the doctor break it again to see if it would heal? No. Rather, the doctor would immobilize it, protect it, and let the healing process take its course.

In contrast, in the case of our mental therapeutic processes, we tend to return again and again to the scene of the injury, re-inflict it, and wonder why recovery is so slow. That's why we need to encourage healing, not analysis.

When explaining the Three Principles, we like to use the example of a hot air balloon.

The balloon possesses a natural buoyancy; it wants to rise. When it's high in the sky, we're well above any obstacles. We can see clearly with a fresh perspective. We can also note any hazards and dangers, so we can take action well before they become a problem. To stop the balloon from rising too fast, we attach weights and sandbags. These are the weights of our negative thinking. When we accumulate too much weight, the balloon starts to descend.

The closer to the ground we are, the more hazardous our circumstances become. The weight of our thinking drags us down. We tend to burn more and more fuel until the weight becomes too much and we crash.

Most people operate in an inefficient high-energy mode. They're weighed down by numerous sandbags, and they burn copious amounts of fuel to compensate. They're in danger of running out of lift. In a hot air balloon, what do you do if you're about to crash? You drop a few sandbags, then drop a few more. Your natural resilience will allow you to rise without effort. That's the CALM approach.

Practical Mindfulness Exercise

Question: Have you ever been under extreme pressure? What happened to get you back to a normal state of mind?

Answer: Recall what you did and how you felt. Think of one or two more instances and repeat the exercise.

You may have noticed that when you take a break from your stressful circumstances, life becomes easier and more pleasurable. Your natural mental healing process kicks in.

The more extreme the pressure, the stronger the push from your innate health will be.

Stress Management by CALM

Earlier, I mentioned the three questions I use as a reminder of the CALM stress-management approach. (If you go to www.thecalmrevolution.com, you can download and carry around a handy wallet-size card listing these questions.) This three-step approach is:

1. Can I change the situation?
2. Can I change my thinking about the situation?
3. Can I remove myself from the situation?

Let's look at these three options more closely.

1. Change the Situation

The simplest and easiest way to remove stress is to remove the stressor. If you're worried about meeting a deadline, can you find a way to make that deadline, or re-negotiate it? If you're worried about a broken relationship, can you repair it? If you're short of money, can you find a way to acquire some? In other words, can you do something to remove or ameliorate the stressor?

When coaching my clients, I continue to be amazed at the number of resourceful, insightful, inspiring ways clients come up with to solve their issues—that is, once they relax a bit and access their innate wisdom.

2. Change Your Thinking

Okay, sometimes you can't come up with an answer that works. You may have tried lots of ways to fix things, but the situation remains at an impasse. Bosses will still be troublesome, customers difficult, family members unappreciative, friends unsupportive. Lovers will leave, children will disappoint, parents will disapprove. In business, people will make poor decisions, blame will be apportioned unfairly, politics will trump ability.

Those situations won't change anytime soon.

Is there any way you can accept what's stressing you and maintain your integrity? People have been given the gift of the Three Principles to create their lives, and yet some make poor choices. Can you accept all people as flawed and see that they, like you, are doing the best they can with what they know? They will make mistakes; you will make mistakes. Your manager, your customers, your suppliers, your staff, your family—all have their own pressures, and they are all trying their best to cope with their lives too.

Remember, people are human and doing the best they can.

3. Remove Yourself from the Situation

If you can't accept a situation, then consider removing yourself from it. You may be in an abusive relationship at work or in your personal life. You may be drowning in stress. You're doing yourself no favors by hanging in there. Despite your immense reserves of resilience, you *can* use them up. If your life is showing a net loss of resilience, it's time to change something.

I saw firsthand the effects of stress on my colleagues—on their health and their relationships. I've felt it myself, but luckily I'm surrounded by supportive friends and family who have helped me through stressful times.

It may seem as if you're stuck, believing you may think you have to keep going in that role because of financial commitments and the expectations of those around you. In truth, the world is one of abundance and possibility. You have only to let go and see it.

Remember this: nothing in this world is worth sacrificing your physical and mental health for. Therefore, choose from the three options you have to free yourself of the burden that's stressing you.

In the next chapter, we'll look at stress's close relative, 'Busyness', and see how CALM can help us there.

CHAPTER 7
Too Busy to Think Straight

The reason for time is so that everything doesn't happen at once.

— Albert Einstein

It was a typical business lunch: the guest of honor was the CEO of a major telecommunications company. He was open and affable, describing the challenges his business faced in a world where traditional voice traffic and revenues were failing, data connectivity had become a commodity, and value added services were being snapped up by smaller, leaner, more agile businesses. He had no easy answers, in a surprising display of frankness. I mused that if I had turned up at a meeting and offered only problems, with no real solutions, my consulting career would have been very short. But many leaders feel that their job is to define the issues, and then get the right people in to provide the solutions.

What struck me however, was how busy he was. The MC was at pains to stress that he had only limited time with us, before rushing off with his team to the airport to a round of meetings in another country. The atmosphere was one of rush, of having so many important things to do.

Afterwards I struck up a conversation with the person next to me. He asked me what I did, and I told him I helped corporate clients find the time and space to think. "Exactly" he said. "We really have that problem. We just don't have time to think." We exchanged business cards. I read his. He was the Asia Pacific CEO of a major consulting firm. It looks like the very people we rely on to solve our business problems suffer from the same problem.

In reality, we have plenty of time to think, but we don't seem to have the time to do the thinking that matters: to provide insight and new ways of solving persistent business problems. It seems the work environment works against us. The sense of urgency, the seeming serious importance of the issues we are facing right now, means that action is imperative. Even if we ourselves achieve a semblance of calm, others around us seem to be able to penetrate this easily with incessant demands. Contemplation is a luxury, to be performed at some time in the future, or on a retreat. Our CEOs, those that are supposed to lead by example, do set an example. They seem to regard time as being so precious we have to fill every second of every day with as much thought as possible. Even when on an executive retreat the agenda tends to be packed, trying to get as much in as possible, aware of the valuable time being eaten up by taking the top team out of the business for a while.

When we investigate with clients when they do their best thinking, the answer seems to be: "Anywhere but at work" - when relaxing, or exercising, or in the shower. Often an insight comes unexpectedly, and importantly, when they weren't aware they were thinking about the problem at all. It's not time to think that's missing at all. It's the mental space not to think, to allow insight to flow freely.

The answer to this issue is surprising, but one we can all recognize. It is not in finding more time, perhaps by exploiting time-management techniques to give us more time to think. I can guarantee that if you do find a good time management technique, you will use up all that extra time in very short order and still be left with that feeling of urgency and busyness. It is difficult to be clear, calm and focused when your mind is still operating at a thousand miles an hour. The answer perhaps is in a surprising direction: pay attention to our mood.

A powerful exercise we run with our clients is our Mood Mapper diagnostic tool. Its aim is to look at the quality of our thinking, not just the quantity. We discover that our mood has a fundamental effect on our sense of time and our ability to deal with our circumstances. We work through the matrix below, looking at how the world appears to us, depending on our mood:

Mood	Time Sense	Circumstances	
Creative, Insightful	Disappears	Exciting, Interesting	
Focused, Aligned	Expands	Opportunities	People, teams and organisations settle into a level that becomes their "normal" state
Calm, Clear	Enough	Straightforward	
Okay, but Stressed	Moving Too fast	Chores, Responsibilities	
Confusion, Frazzled	Crisis, Urgent	Obstacles, Threats	
Despair, Resignation	A Never Ending Burden	Impossible	

It appears that the lighter our mood, the more time we feel we have. When the mood is heavy and serious we are acutely aware of time, and we don't feel we have enough. When our mood lightens, we don't feel the pressure of time anymore, but even more importantly, we look at our circumstances as being full of opportunities and challenges, not obstacles and threats.

And who sets the mood of the organization? You guessed it. Those at the top.

Putting this sense of busyness through the Insight Generator produces similar interesting results, this time about the thoughts we are holding onto that are causing this situation:

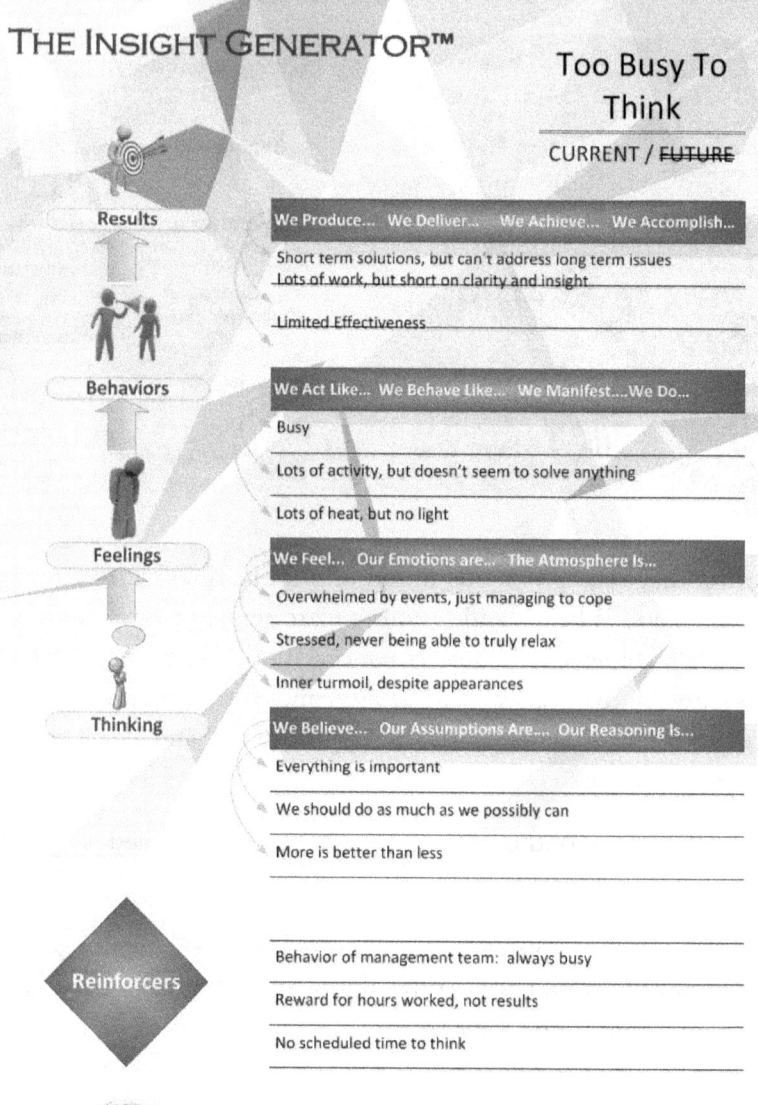

Chapter 7: Too Busy to Think Straight 109

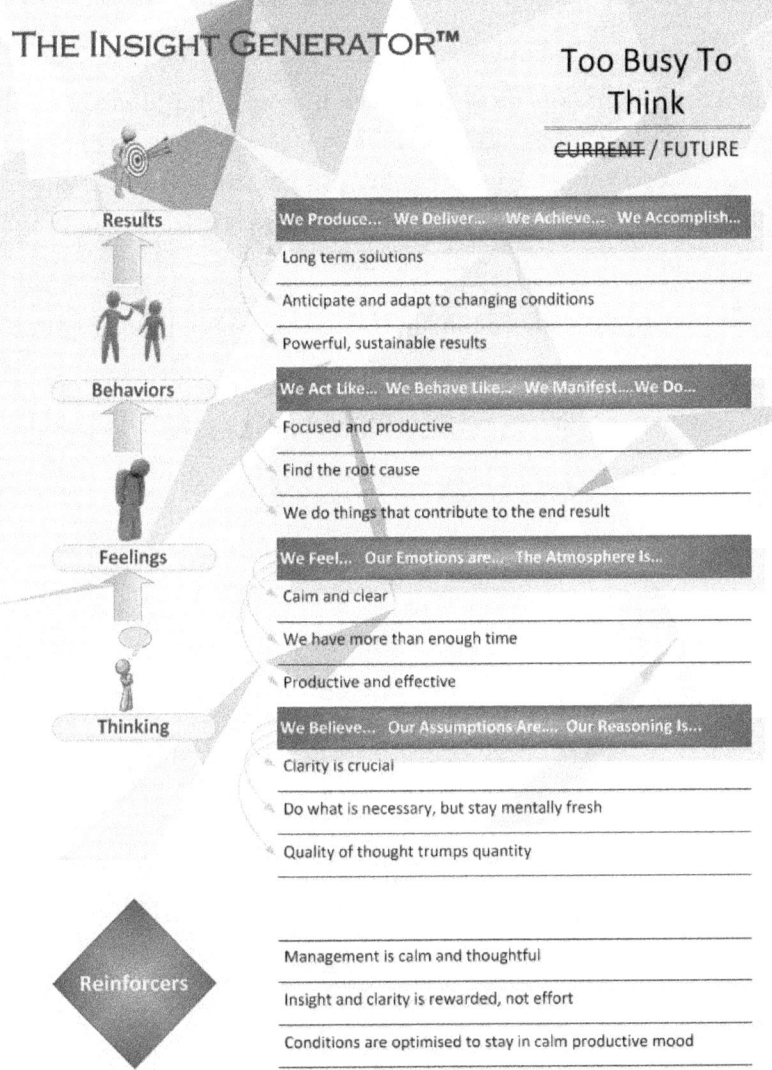

We could teach all sorts of time-management techniques, but we guarantee that within a week you will be just as busy as before, simply because you haven't dealt with the root cause. Stephen Covey has addressed this in the third of the Seven Habits of Highly Effective People: "Put first things first."[14]

The aim is to focus on those activities that are 'Important' and 'Not Urgent'. These activities are the building blocks that enable you to succeed. However, in our business life, it's common to value busyness over effectiveness. But have you noticed? The best leaders never seem rushed or stressed, even in perilous times.

But the two words of advice remain if you want more time. Lighten up!

In the next chapter we are going to look at how a sense of calm enables us to effectively plan for the future, in an exercise called: From There to Here

---

[14] Stephen R. Covey. *Seven Habits of Highly Effective People*. Simon & Schuster, 2000

CHAPTER 8
From There to Here

From there to here, and here to there, funny things are everywhere.

– Dr. Seuss

I am a fan of Dr. Seuss's light-hearted, amusing, almost nonsensical approach to the world that also evokes underlying wisdom. Anyone who has had to work in a team-building exercise appreciates the moral of the star-bellied sneeches.

Dr. Seuss' books gave rise to another powerful exercise that helps people turn plans into action. Most plans start from *here* and go *there*. In managing projects, we discovered that if we started *there* and worked our way back to *here*, things made far more sense. That way we could see why we were doing things in the way we proposed.

In my years of working in project management, I advanced through the ranks until I either ran complex programs of work or put them back on track. I always met resistance from the project team and the target organization regarding what we were doing and when we were going to do it. The usual refrain was, "We don't have enough time (or money or resources) to do this."

At times the resistance got quite sophisticated. They'd say, "We couldn't do this because we didn't have a particular tool or process." People who took this approach spent a lot of time developing detailed analyses of why failure had been assured! This generally indicted the organization's change-resistant state of mind.

Have you ever worked on a project for which the team thought there was enough time, resources, or knowledge to deliver the end product? That said, my teams have delivered plenty of projects on time, to spec, and under budget, despite initial concerns. So I learned firsthand the perils of trying to get something done in any organization. As humans, it's easier for others to criticize than to constructively help the effort. This attitude of resistance reflected that of an often-skeptical senior management team.

As time went by, I discovered that many of the arguments concerned the basic processes we were using to run a project, what form the deliverables would take, and when they should be delivered. This resistance occurred at many levels, including that of the steering committee, which caused me to redouble my efforts to keep things moving. In those cases, I had to start from the beginning and clearly define project methodology and exact details. After all, that was my area of expertise, so I had to deliver it.

The Resistance Continued

My efforts though were to no avail. Again and again, the resistance continued, fueled by fear of the unknown or what seemed like willful ignorance. It wasn't until I worked with a dear colleague, Robyn Pagonis—the most gifted change manager I've ever met—that we solved the puzzle together. The root cause was this: *When people don't understand something, they just say no.*

If we go back to the CALM approach, we can run this idea through the Insight Generator. The Three Principles take us back to the idea that *people are always trying to work things out for themselves. If they don't have the opportunity to work things out at a pace they're comfortable with, they'll keep on resisting.*

So even when it comes to a well-known methodology such as a System Development Life Cycle (SDLC), plenty of room remains for people to interpret it differently. For example, try getting someone to define the difference between System Testing, System Integration Testing, and User Acceptance Testing. Not easy.

So Robin and I started to run our project planning a different way, using the techniques described here. We witnessed these astounding outcomes:

- Team members inexperienced in software development or business change came up with an approach that looked almost exactly like the standard methodology. This time, they bought into it *because they had thought it through themselves.*

- The business change activities that teams suggested occupied center stage and reflected a sophisticated knowledge of how to make things work in the organization. After all, they were experts in their own company.

- The outcome was far better than an individual project manager could come up with on his or her own.

- Resistance turned into cooperation and innovation.

We called this approach "From There to Here," and it's become our standard project-planning approach.

From There to Here Exercise

To set the scene of the meeting, use your Practical Mindfulness skills to get everyone comfortable: Be calm yourself, ask what is going on for them, then:

1. Ask if anyone has any burning issues. Write these down on a chart and keep it on the wall. If the questions can be quickly answered, do so; but if not, don't get bogged down. Move on. Politely.

2. Ask "What does success look like?" Normally participants will struggle at first, but if you allow them the mental space to work it out, you will find they will become quite enthusiastic. Use your new listening skills to give them time and space to mindfully respond. This is an important question. Most projects fail because people had differing ideas of what it was supposed to deliver.

3. Ask "How will we know when it's finished?" and record the replies. Notice the mindset will have already changed from a frightening near future to a glorious success.

4. Draw up a timeline from now until the expected finish.

5. Ask everyone to brainstorm all the things to be done and write them on sticky notes. Allow them to do this in a way that's comfortable for them—on their own or in groups. If they're having trouble, get them to work backward from the successful outcome.

6. Get the participants, in turn, to place their notes on the timeline, explaining what each activity is. It is important to get them to do this themselves. Allow discussion. It is tempting to do it for them, especially if you are an experienced project manager, but this will turn it from their plan to your plan, with consequent lack of ownership.

7. Draw "buckets" around activities in a common group.

8. Following the discussion, run another round asking if anyone has missed anything.

9. Ask if any key relationships exist between the activities, e.g., design before development, testing

before deployment. Then draw the arrows.

10. Ask who should be responsible for each task.

11. Ask what needs to happen in one week, one month, three months.

12. Take a photo of the timeline and document the tasks, owners, and dates, and then distribute.

13. Take a well-earned rest. Your project is well on its way to success.

This "There to Here" exercise is the cornerstone of our 3Rs approach to project recovery. The 3Rs are:

1. Root Cause: Find out the Root Cause of the issues. Don't only treat the symptoms; ascertain the root causes of issues and address them.

2. Rebuild the Relationships: Almost every troubled project is characterized by broken relationships. These have to be rebuilt for progress to be made.

3. Restart or Retire the Project: Get the project back on track by restarting it on a proper basis, or close it down if it's clear it's not going to work.

It's fun to restart a project on a proper footing. Better yet, if it was run well at the *outset* of an initiative, you wouldn't even need recovery.

Not Everyone Has the Same Picture

Mainly, the exercise recognizes a simple Practical Mindfulness fact: *That we're all working things out for ourselves.* Each person's experience feels absolutely real to that individual, so it's easy to *assume* everyone else has exactly the same view. It feels so real. But let me assure you, even for the simplest project, views differ greatly, and these differences constitute the source of much tension. What other people are doing doesn't make sense to us in terms of our own picture, which is painted courtesy of our individual use of the principles of Mind, Thought, and Consciousness. We may think others are misguided, stubborn, resistant, or even stupid. Instead, they're acting with impeccable logic in terms of their own view of things. Remember, behaviors and results represent the logical outcome of each person's underlying thinking.

Therefore, successful leaders set the conditions by which people can do two things: 1) work things out for themselves and 2) develop a shared understanding with everyone else.

The worst way to manage a project is to simply *tell* others what to do. I have no idea why this approach remains so popular. Perhaps it's the fastest way and time is precious. But usually huge amounts of effort go into preparing elaborate presentations and analyses to persuade people to take action through rational thought. With a little more time and Practical Mindfulness, much less effort produces a far better understanding that endures.

Practical Mindfulness Exercise

Question: Under what conditions do you learn best?

Advanced question: What's the best way to get people to work something out for themselves?

I hope you smiled because you now know the answer. People learn best when they feel calm, open, and safe. Therefore, the best way to get people to work things out for themselves is to ask a question. The act of answering causes them to dip into their innate wisdom—the place from which answers arise.

CHAPTER 9
Clarity is the Key

One cool judgment is worth a thousand hasty counsels. The thing to do is to supply light and not heat.

– Woodrow T. Wilson

When taking over a project, among the first things I'd hear was this: "We have no project plan." In fact, there always *was* a project plan—usually long, detailed, and complex. Whenever I started a project myself, I'd often hear this same complaint about the specifications, design, and key building blocks.

So I'd confront the people citing the physical plan and their response would be, "Oh, that! That's not a real project plan. It doesn't make sense." What they really meant was, "I don't understand what my role in the project is and what's expected of me." They did understand, though, that they weren't allowed to state it or didn't want to admit it.

Consider this: The traditional gantt chart with many lines of activites is *not* a good way of communicating to team members what needs to happen. However, it's a highly effective way for a project manager to work out what needs to happen. It forces the project manager to go through the thought process of analysis and planning. Instead, you'd require simpler approaches that allow people to work out details in specific areas for themselves.

The project recovery process involved taking the heat out of the situation and restoring it to normality so people could start thinking straight again. That's the entire basis of Practical Mindfulness and the CALM approach.

Management 101

A popular message that attendees request at my presentations is the

> ### Management 101
>
> 1. Does everyone know what it is they are supposed to be doing?
> 2. Has everyone agreed to do it?
> 3. Does everyone know how to do it?
> 4. Are they doing it effectively?
>
>

following:

This simple "Management 101" checklist has stood me in good stead. Whenever I did a project recovery, I'd discover that despite the processes, procedures, and documentation, any problems in project execution stemmed from a basic lack of clarity in what we were building and who was building it.

It's the same in any business endeavor; people tend to get so busy they have no mental space to work things through so that they are clear. A frenzied project situation just makes things worse.

This chapter provides four Practical Mindfulness approaches to getting things done. The first is making sure people know what they are supposed to do; the second is making sure they agree to do it; the third is making sure they know how to do it, and the fourth is making sure they continue to do it effectively. Sounds simple, I know. The truth *is* simple. Yet, overlooking these four check-in questions is the root cause of most project issues.

Knowing What to Do

The project manager's bible is the *Project Management Body of Knowledge* (PMBOK). Now in its fifth edition, its 589 pages contain 47 separate processes for managing projects. I know because I became a certified Project Management Professional (PMP). I had to pass a test on its contents as well as demonstrate I had at least 4,500 hours under my belt as a project manager. I discovered the easiest way to pass the test was to learn every process, every input, every technique, every output. The rational mind does have its uses.

The problem? Although I was a certified PMP, few of the team members were also certified. But I still needed them to run their part of the project in accordance with the agreed-upon processes. The existence of PMBOK's detailed project processes implied that managing was a difficult, academically-demanding exercise.

However, project management as a discipline has only been formally recognized since the 1950s. Pyramids have been built, navies launched, armadas repulsed, nuclear bombs built—all without the aid of a PMP. And by the time the Project Management Institute was formed in 1969, man had already successfully landed on the moon.

In my view, managing projects isn't all that difficult (as the PMBOK implies); therefore, I had to find ways to communicate what was required to my team members in simple terms.

We don't have time to communicative effectively.

When starting a new initiative, one of the first things we're taught to do is conduct a project definition workshop. In a number of projects I have led, I've experienced staunch resistance to this. First is the feeling we just don't have time for these things. We need to take action, not sit around talking. "There is no need," the sponsor may say. "We have been working on the business case for two years. Everyone is clear!"

But I've learned that you absolutely *have* to conduct a definition workshop. One of the first exercises is a variation of 'From There to Here.' We go around the room and ask everyone, one by one, what the project is producing. The first person asked makes a statement, but already a disagreement shows up. Then we invite the second person to comment. That person's viewpoint is always different than the first person's. Always. By the time the third person provides input, those in the room are *starting* to understand the idea. That's when their annoyance in thinking the others have got it wrong turns to amused understanding. Clearly, each individual has his or her view of what's going on.

Why had the sponsor resisted the idea of the workshop, saying it wasn't necessary? Because he was clear on the objectives. And when he asked others whether they were clear, they said yes. Certainly in their own minds, they were clear, too.

It's just that everyone's clear view was different!

Traditional means of communicating—PowerPoint presentations, specifications, long documents, etc.—essentially go in one direction. They don't allow for people to interact and *develop their own understanding*. Understanding comes from dialogue, not just talking, and not just listening. The problems of one-way communication are well understood, yet the methods described remain surprisingly popular. Why? Because people believe they don't have time to hold definition meetings. What are they actually saying?

We don't have time to communicate effectively.

This simple misconception has been the cause of more project problems than anything else. You don't get better communication by talking faster. Nor do you get more understanding and insight by providing as much one-way input as possible.

When you are calm—and *stay* calm—that's when effective communication occurs.

Having ownership is the key

Ensuring that people take ownership of their tasks becomes the most important day-to-day management activity for leaders. Many project managers draw up an RACI matrix (Responsible, Accountable, Consulted, Involved) so people identify their roles and claim their responsibilities for each task. A debate then ensues about the difference between being responsible and accountable.

To this day, I've never seen that debate end. Plus, most people prefer to be consulted or informed rather than take responsibility for actually producing something. But that attitude doesn't get anything done!

However, people understand the concept of ownership. One person becomes the owner of the task, the one to ensure it gets completed. That's it. If the task doesn't have someone who acknowledges ownership, it almost certainly won't get done. Likewise, if the ownership is shared, it probably won't get done either.

Make sure every task is owned, and owned by one person only.

Knowing How to Do It

Almost every manager has also been a student. And every student knows the experience of having to make deadlines and missing them. In the project management canon, this experience is called the student syndrome. The following diagram illustrates this disorder:

When we are first assigned a task, we typically take a look at it and then decide when we will do it. Being busy, we usually choose to do it later. Then, as the deadline approaches, we pick it up and start working on it. That's when we discover it's not as clear-cut as we first thought. We have to put in a lot of effort at the end, delivering a result that's rushed and often late. Does this sound familiar?

Experienced managers are aware of this part of human nature. So, rather than putting the pressure on time creating more rushed results, they try to deepen the understanding of those responsible about exactly *how* to do the task. They investigate early with those responsible; they understand that, although we like to think we know everything, everyone is constantly working out how to do things as they go along.

Staying on Track

Rule number one is this: *There will always be problems.*

In my experience, dealing with obstacles requires us to *be in the right mindset,* so we can overcome them. Therefore, our mindset—the essence of the CALM approach—is key to our success. As we can see from Chapter 5 on Mood, keeping your own mood in a light-hearted, easy space allows insight to flourish.

When we are calm, insight can occur, and problems can be solved.

Yet, when we are stressed, problems seem insurmountable. There seems to be only one solution to any particular issue—or no solution at all.

What is the solution? Keep the mood light. That's when a multitude of solutions and even opportunities can become apparent.

Facing Project Management Challenges

The following points summarize what typically happens in a project:

> The reason for any business problem is deceptively complex and surprisingly simple—that is, people don't have a full picture of what is going on.

> When people don't understand, they say no. This is the cause of all resistance.

People are working things out for themselves. Help them do it.

If an activity is not owned, it won't get done.

If someone doesn't know he or she is supposed to do it, it won't get done. Are you sure you actually asked them to do it?

People operate best in a calm environment.

An issue is caused by holding onto thinking. Use CALM to establish what that thinking is and allow better thinking to shine through.

Four Basic Items

When we are calm, our insights and understanding of these four basic Management 101 questions can evolve:

1. Does everyone know what it is they are supposed to be doing?
2. Has everyone agreed to do it?
3. Does everyone know how to do it?
4. Are they doing it effectively?

The best managers approach their work on the basis of these basic items, and constantly revisit them as an ongoing process.

CALM Mindset

What does a CALM mindset mean for you and your organization?

1. The root CAUSE of project failure is thinking that all participants know what they are doing.

2. If we are AWARE that everyone by definition has an individual view, we will make more time to ensure we develop a consistent, collective view.

3. To get that collective view, we need to LET GO of our individual views.

4. Keeping the MOOD light results in better decisions and better execution.

CHAPTER 10
Meetings Transformed

A successful meeting is one in which the participants accomplish the purpose of the meeting and feel uplifted and better connected.

– Robert Kausen

Robert Kausen has written the seminal book on how to stage successful meetings: *We've Got to Start Meeting Like This!*[15] By now, it won't surprise you to learn that the first half of the book is his explanation of the Three Principles. He then focuses on applying these principles to one of the most time-consuming activities in our business life: meetings.

While structure as well as punctuality is important for meetings, Kausen focuses on one key element: the tone of the meeting, defined as the sum of the individual states of mind.

Think of a great meeting. What happened? What was the atmosphere, the tone? Think of a meeting that wasn't so great. What was the tone there? What was the result? What was the feeling of the participants as

---

15   Robert C. Kausen. *We've Got To Start Meeting Like This! How to Get Better Results with Fewer Meetings.* Life Education, Inc., 2003.

they left the room? Chances are you'd agree with him!

Kausen provides the following correlation between the tone of the meeting and the quality of thinking involved.[16]

Meeting Tone	Quality of Thinking
Exhilarating	Brilliant
Inspiring	Insightful
Uplifting	Creative
Enjoyable	Collaborative
Neutral	Cooperative
Tense	Defensive
Stressed	Argumentative
Adversarial	Reactive
Bogged Down	Dull
Discouraging	Grinding

It is debatable whether the quality of thinking created the tone, or the tone created the quality of thinking. They are both representative of the Three Principles at work. One thing is for sure though, when the tone is poor, the results are poor.

---

16   Robert Kausen, *We've Got to Start Meeting Like This!* p.79.

Chapter 10: Meetings Transformed

Letting Go of Control

Having heard me speak at an industry conference my client, Phil, had recommended me to his organization. I was hired to deliver a keynote speech and run a workshop at a two-day conference for 800 of his company's managers. I was happy he was now asking me to join him for coffee because I enjoy keeping in touch with clients.

Over coffee, Phil told me this story: He was a project manager running a difficult project. Key stakeholders held a weekly meeting that was always stressful. Then he and his colleague had attended my workshop and loved it. He wanted to find ways to put the Three Principles into action in his company.

"It was amazing." he said. "We normally dreaded the meeting and put all sorts of effort into trying to manage it so it didn't spiral out of control. After your workshop, we did nothing. It's hard to explain, but we just turned up. We didn't do anything special. We weren't even trying to listen. We kept our minds clear, and the meeting went smoothly. People caught the spirit of calm and participated in a normal way. This stuff really works."

In my workshop with Phil's company, and others, I didn't talk about meeting structures or formal approaches. Rather than that, I discussed the influence our thinking has on our own actions and on others' actions, too. Phil and his colleagues simply worked it out from there.

No Longer Rushed and Flustered

I was running a major time-critical project that required two senior execs to attend weekly status meetings. The organization had a culture of immediate action rather than thoughtful consideration. The execs typically arrived 10 minutes late, feeling rushed and flustered. They knew this meeting was important, but they'd already sat in on two of a similar nature that morning.

How do you think the meeting went?

Another company had a chairman who never seemed flustered. He greeted us warmly as we came in the door. We got the sense that he trusted us and valued our input, and he knew he had to rely on us.

How do you think *that* meeting went?

One of the biggest problems facing our clients is a culture of meetings that don't work. Let's see what happens if we put this situation through the CALM approach.

Current State		Desired State
• Team meetings often do not accomplish their objectives due to lack of structure in and conversations that drag on • Team members are frustrated with and cynical about working with each other	RESULTS	• Team meetings accomplish their objectives as conversations are effective and well managed • Team members enjoy working with each other
• Piling on issues during a conversation • Frequent interruptions • Listening not actively practiced • Most statements begin with 'no' or 'but'	ACTIONS	• Conversations are driven to their logical end one by one • No interruptions • Reflective listening is employed • Statements begin with liaisons
• Anxious to speak and get a word in • Uncomfortable letting the same individuals always speak • Angry that no one will listen	FEELINGS	• Curious about the conversation • Honoring what others are saying • Assured that voice will be heard
• If I do not jump in, no one will listen to me • Every one thinks their point of view is best and must defend their opinion to succeed • No one cares about what others think	THINKING	• If I do not speak, there is a strong chance that what I wanted to say will be said • I will get a chance to share my thoughts • Everyone cares about what others have to say
• Leadership role models poor team meeting behaviors • No meeting training • No feedback is ever given to anyone regarding their communication behaviors • No performance management around collaboration	Reinforcers	• Leadership runs excellent meetings • Meeting training is offered to everyone • Feedback regarding communication behaviors is permitted and given • Collaboration is formally reviewed during each performance review

Chapter 10: Meetings Transformed   131

Here's how it works with the Mood Mapper.

MOOD MAPPER™ Domain: *Listening*

State of Mind	My Experience	Impact
Passionate	Highly Attentive, Broader Perspective, Overly Optimistic, Hearing only the positive	Creative, Inspiring, but ignoring real problems that may exist. Pie in the sky
Confident	Curiosity, Focused, Engaged Listening, Active Listening, Caring	Insights abound, mood lifts, solutions come easily, motivating
Calm	Present and attentive, Empathetic listener, Receptive listening	Calming, Sensible, Steadies the ship, Its not so difficult
Anxious	Lack of Focus, Impatient, Interrogative question, pre-occupied and distracted	Demotivating, not interested, troubles seem real. Go away and work it out later
Discouraged	Closed, Argumentative, Critical and Judgmental, Detached, Misinterpretations	More problems occur, lack of trust, things get worse. Get stuck too.
Defeated	Inability to listen, Caught up in own stuff, Can only hear what's wrong Uninterested	Moaning Minnie, Depressing, We're doomed, nothing can be done..

www.thecalmrevolution.com

Based on the exercise States of Mind and used by permission of the Accompli Group

Set the Tone

Key to this practical approach is conducting great meetings—getting the state of mind right and focusing on the tone. To help people run successful meetings, I take them through the following steps:

1. The meeting has started before it begins. Sometimes it started in the elevator to the meeting room or in the corridor. As soon as people come in the door, make personal contact with them. Greet them. Acknowledge their presence. Talk to them.

2. Get everyone engaged early. This may take more time than you prepared for, but it's vital. Give attendees a chance to talk right away. Ask them how the situation looks to them, if they have any burning issues, what they want to get out of the meeting.

3. Set an example by listening respectfully. Help the participants understand issues at a deeper level to get to the root cause of the problem. *Insight trumps all.* So don't rush too quickly to action if the causes of the issue aren't clear. People tend to go to an intellectual view too early.

4. Draw out knowledge from participants who may not have volunteered information. The introverted, introspective members of the team need to be given an opening in which to speak. Give them permission to contribute if that's what they're waiting

for. It's worth it; they're the ones who think things through before they talk.

5. Influence the meeting for the better, even if you're not the leader. Pay attention to the tone. If the energy drops, intervene by asking questions of people or seek clarification: e.g., "What do you think the real problem is here?"

6. Set a good example by your actions and your thoughtfulness.

7. Be sure to come up with a better solution than if you had not met. Remember, that's why you had the meeting in the first place.

CHAPTER 11
Putting Off Procrastination

Procrastination is my sin. It brings me naught but sorrow. I know that I should stop it. In fact, I will—tomorrow.

– Gloria Pitzer

I suffer from procrastination, and it seems everyone I discuss it with suffers from it too. For example, it took me eight years to write my first book, and then I wrote the second one in only 10 days. What happened in between? I "ate my own cooking" and applied the CALM approach.

Procrastination is a heavy feeling, weighted with thought. People assume they're lazy and need to force themselves to get something done. By examining this assumption with the understanding of how our thinking works, we discover we're not lazy at all. Procrastination is hard work—and quite creative. It seems there's no end to the amusements and distractions we can involve ourselves in to avoid doing what we have to do. This isn't fun. It's terrible.

Plus, the more important things are to us in general, the more susceptible they are to debilitating procrastination. Let's look at the reasons why.

With procrastination, people have two competing sets of thoughts: 1) The set of positive thoughts that tell us the good reasons we should do something and 2) something else that holds us back. This brings us back to driving the car while pressing both the accelerator and the brake pedal at the same time. Clearly, applying more energy delivers more heat but not more progress.

It's possible to force ourselves through a task by emphasizing the good reasons, getting motivated, and being accountable. But then the "something else" gets stronger, too.

I discovered the "something else" at a meeting of the International Coaching Federation. The speaker gave a clear and insightful talk on how procrastination, or any lack of action, is due to competing thoughts. So far, so good. He then stated it would take an intensive 10-month coaching process to find out what those thoughts were. I turned to my partner in the exercise and got the answer in two minutes. I asked, "What stops us doing what we are supposed to do?"

Let's put this question through the Insight Generator:

Chapter 11: Putting Off Procrastination 137

THE INSIGHT GENERATOR™

Writing a book

CURRENT / ~~FUTURE~~

Results — We Produce... We Deliver... We Achieve... We Accomplish...
- Lots of basic material, but no structure
- 75 pages so far of unstructured material
- Lots of source material and images (it's a start!)

Behaviors — We Act Like... We Behave Like... We Manifest...We Do...
- False starts, many re-starts with great effort
- Procrastination, keep on putting it off
- Lots of talk but no action

Feelings — We Feel... Our Emotions are... The Atmosphere Is...
- Congestion, frustration, self-loathing at inability to get it done
- Knowing its important, but unable to do anything about it
- Fantasy and fear combined: it will be great, but it may not work

Thinking — We Believe... Our Assumptions Are... Our Reasoning Is...
- I am at risk of utter failure
- I must work it our myself, no one can help me
- I am a true procrastinator and it will be my downfall

Reinforcers
- Advisers say a book is the key to success, but there is a lot of vanity press out there
- No one is offering help that makes sense
- People ask "When is the book coming out?"

www.thecalmrevolution.com   Based on the exercise "The Thinking Path" by the Accompli Group

Hmmm, interesting so far. Particularly the fear. I hadn't admitted it to myself until someone did me the service of listening to me and drew it out.

What could I possibly be afraid of? This chart revealed a lot.

Good Reasons for Book	Counteracting Fear
Bring fundamental understanding of how we work to a lot more people	Open myself up to ridicule
Change the world	Be ignored by the world
Do rewarding work	Find no one understands what I'm writing about
Meet my business goals	All those plans may not come to fruition

It makes sense: If everything is a result of thought, we must have negative thoughts as well as positive thoughts, so perhaps the more important something is to us, the more we fear failing.

Many people try to power themselves through procrastination by increasing their motivation, but this can lead to more resistance in a vicious cycle. As we saw in the hot air balloon analogy, we can go for the strategy of *overpowering our negative thinking* by putting forward a lot of energy, or we can drop unhelpful thoughts like sandbags.

So, first I faced my fears (as noted in the chart). Once they were out in the open, they couldn't hold their grip on me for long. Then I joined an authorship mastermind group and received both moral and practical support. After that, a development editor contacted me and offered me assistance. I finally got writing and finished the book, but with mixed results. This chart explains a bit more.

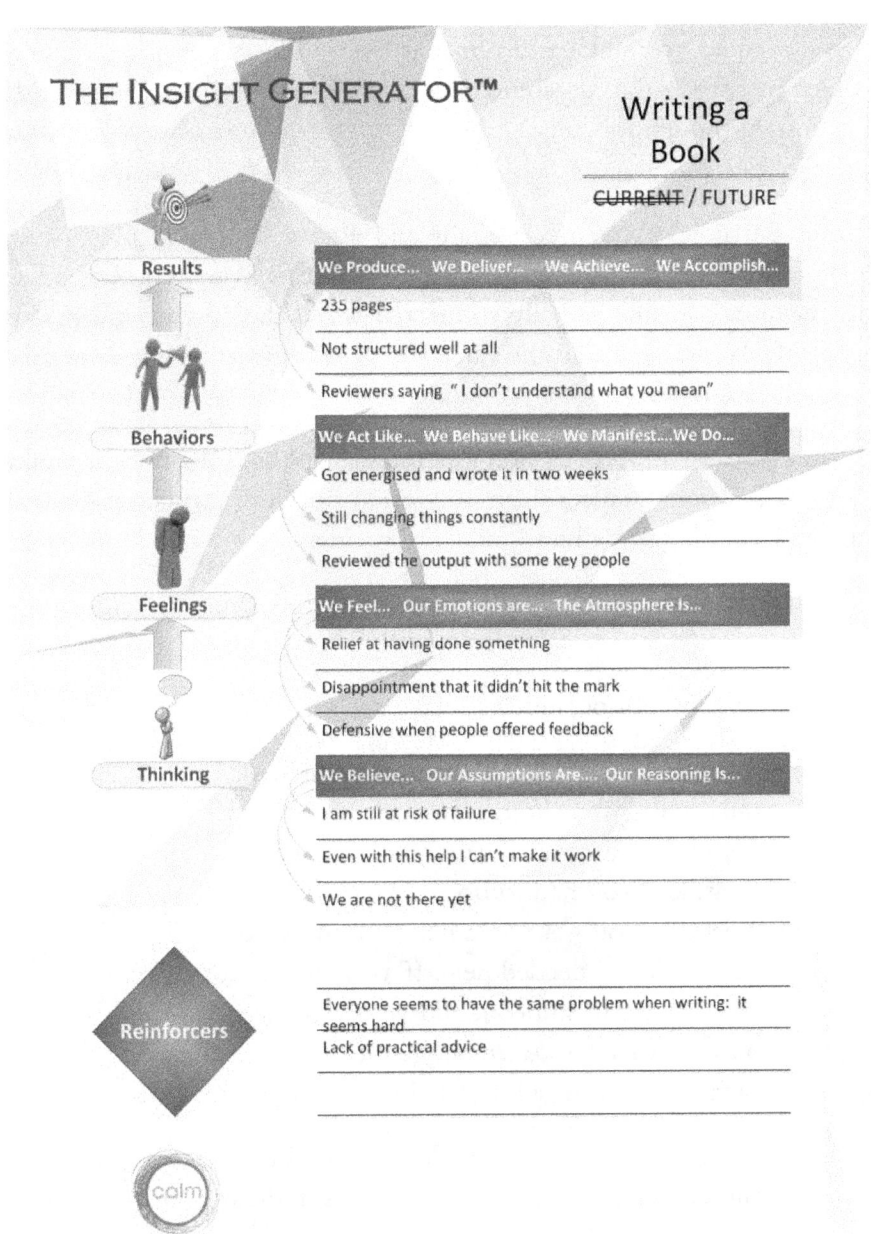

I had made progress and proven I wasn't a chronic procrastinator, plus I received interest and encouragement. However, I still had work to do.

Let's consider my thinking this time around: I was still at risk of failure, which meant I had to do something more. I was on the right track. My big insight though was this: *If I'm not getting the right results, I'm not getting the right help.*

Enter Raymond Aaron, consultant and author of *Double Your Income Doing What You Love: Raymond Aaron's Guide to Power Mentoring*. According to Raymond, in this globally connected world the best of the best is available to everyone, and the value you get is normally far greater than even the second best.

Raymond treats procrastination as a useful sign that something is amiss. It's a natural defense mechanism to prevent you from 1) doing the wrong thing or 2) doing something you're not good at.

His advice? If you're not good at something, find someone who *is* good at it.

> From his eBook, here's his take on delegation:
>
>> . . . [Y]ou were misled throughout school. In school, you were given homework in every subject. Some subjects you excelled at and some you were mediocre at. Regardless, you had to do your own homework in each subject. If you got some help, you were admitting you were weak and needed help. If you got a lot of help (in other words, if someone did your homework for you), you were called a *cheater*. So, getting a little help was not macho and getting a lot of help was dishonest.[17]

Unfortunately, this attitude is still alive and well in business today. So I took Raymond's advice. I've noted the results in the chart that follows.

Rather than problems to overcome, procrastination and its younger

---

17   Raymond Aaron. *Double Your Income Doing What You Love*. Nook Book, p. 56.

Chapter 11: Putting Off Procrastination 141

sibling, resistance, become welcome messengers. They tell you something is wrong, but it's not a character defect. That means it's time to use CALM and discover your fears and see what you need to let go of to achieve your goals.

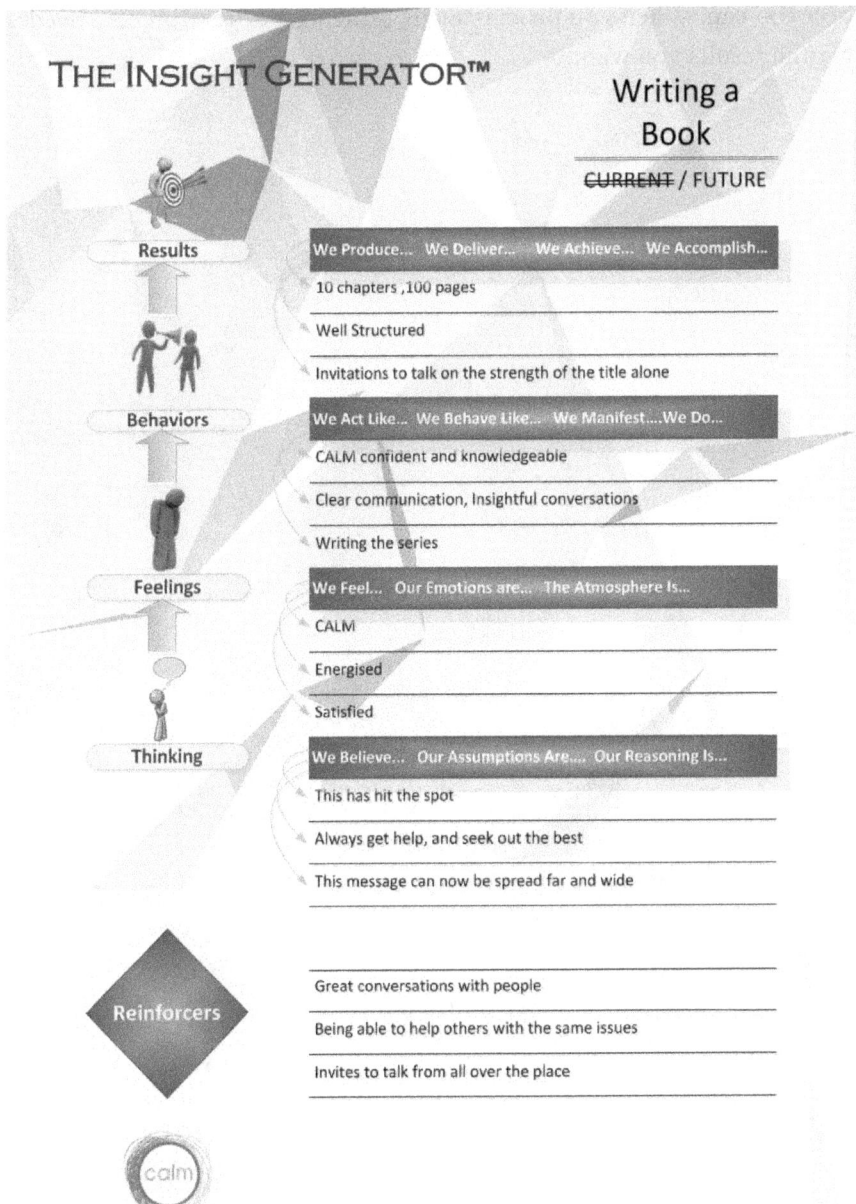

In this case, my fear was that I was not a good enough writer. So I delegated turning a rough draft into a polished piece to my editor, Barbara McNichol. I could have revised and revised this book forever and still not get the result I wanted. Barbara is brilliant at what she does, reinforcing the idea of always using the best you can, not just doing the best you can. When you procrastinate, bring in the "reinforcers" needed for the results you want.

PART III:

Wrap-up

CHAPTER 12
Pollyanna Was Right

I never want to hear from any cheerful Pollyannas who tell me fate supplies a mate. That's all bananas.

– "But Not for Me" (song) George and Ira Gershwin

You may think the CALM approach sounds too simple to be true, and it *is* simple. A good answer is always simple when you view complex issues as many simple issues tied together.

From the presentations and consulting that I do, I anticipate you might be asking the following questions. Let me answer them here.

1. This all sounds very Pollyanna-like. It's not real. People aren't that nice and they don't always act from the best motives.

> If you're unfamiliar with the term Pollyanna, it stems from the novel *Pollyanna*, written in 1913. The novel's success brought the Pollyanna Principle into our language. It refers to someone who seems to always find something to be glad or positive about, no matter the circumstance. The concept is sometimes used pejoratively, referring to someone whose optimism is excessive to the point of naïveté, or who refuses to accept the facts of an

unfortunate situation. The point is, in the novel, everyone comes around to Pollyanna's optimistic, apparently naïve point of view.

With regard to the Three Principles, you have a choice. You can either look for the good in things, or look for the bad. You can appeal to hope or appeal to fear, though the basis of looking for the good (rather than being glib or superficial) results in a profound understanding of humankind's true nature. And that nature is complete and whole.

2. Surely bad people are around, so don't we have to be on our guard?

Indeed, people have a choice how they use the Three Principles, and many people make bad choices, usually through ignorance of how the concepts work. You've learned how thought creates our personal reality and how you can make choices to keep yourself safe. Remember, you're not a prisoner of your thoughts; you *can* change them. So you never have to stay in a situation in which people want you to be a prisoner of *their* thoughts.

3. I would love to be calm, but my company has a culture of busyness. It would be detrimental to my career if I appeared relaxed and not busy.

Take a good look at those people in your organization who are truly successful in all aspects of their lives. Do they appear busy minded? Also look at those who make a big thing about being busy. Are they being truly effective?

A recent study shows that calmness is a key attribute of successful people.[18] If you look carefully, you'll notice a lot of people who are being calmly successful and don't feel the need to make a big noise about it.

---

18   http://www.forbes.com/sites/travisbradberry/2014/02/06/how-successful-people-stay-calm/

In Jim Collins's book *From Good to Great,* the author discusses what he calls fifth-level leadership—the highest level—in which leaders have the qualities of humility combined with strong will. They may not be in the news headlines, but they're greatly respected and get the best results. Why? They're calm, authentic, focused, and centered.

4. You emphasize formless concepts such as thought. Surely form is important; otherwise nothing would get done.

At the root level, there's no difference. Everything is made of the same thing: mind, thought, and consciousness. Form and formlessness are manifestations of these, so I suggest paying attention to both.

In business life, it's often assumed the only thing that matters is the form—or specifically, the results. The assumption is that this is the only thing that is important. However, results consist of many things that are formless in nature, and in the end reveal themselves in a feeling: we feel good about something. Process and procedure definitely have their place, and I've recommended a few I find especially useful—The Insight Generator, Mood Mapper, Stress Approach. That said, be sure to use them mindfully and especially be aware of the underlying thinking.

5. Your approach is quasi-scientific mumbo-jumbo and not provable. It's not rational, and rationality is the key.

If it works, what's the problem? That's proof enough for me—and I hope for you, too.

6. What about the brain? It has a powerful effect, and your rationale could be all in your head.

The brain does indeed have a powerful effect. If the brain is damaged, either physically or by habitual negative thinking, your experience will be affected. However, the brain can change in accordance with the thoughts you emphasize. The 'plasticity' of the brain—its ability to reconfigure itself and form new neural pathways—is better understood today than in the past. *You* choose the thoughts that create those new pathways. Do they take you where you want to go? You get to decide for yourself.

7. One's apparent consciousness is simply the result of chemical reactions and electrical activity in the brain, correct?

You need the Three Principles of Mind, Consciousness, and Thought to even pose that question. Where consciousness comes from is not a question with an answer. It is simply one of the building blocks of our experience, like Mind and Thought. It is not created by anything, or caused by anything. It doesn't exist separately from anything else. Considerable effort has been expended in the field or neuro-science to find consciousness as a separate entity. Yet strangely we are using our consciousness as an integral part of our search. There is no doubt that the state of our brain has an impact on our experience, but to assume it is the source of our experience is a mistake. Rather than investigating the brain, and embuing it with all sorts of mystical properties, consider the source of those properties, and investigate there. I would say the most important thing you could ever learn is understanding that all your experiences are simply how you use the divine gifts of Mind, Consciousness, and Thought to create your world.

That's the basis of the CALM approach to life:

1. Understand the CAUSE of your thinking.

2. Be AWARE of how your thinking works.

3. LET GO of unhelpful thinking by LISTENING to each other.

4. Find that great MOOD.

EPILOGUE

Another flight, another conference. I was getting nonchalant. I still enjoy the thrill of flying. To me it's the most incredible thing; to accelerate powerfully down the runway, soar into the sky, cruise among the clouds. I do my best thinking high up in the sky. Away from distractions and interruptions, I am free to relax and let my mind wander at peace.

Except this time, we didn't seem to be accelerating correctly. No matter how many take-offs we experience, there is always that nagging doubt: "Will we get off the ground?" It adds to the excitement—and to the relief—when we actually do get off the ground.

I told myself not to be silly, a groundless fear . . . then we heard a bang and felt a lurch, and the airplane started braking heavily. Not good. An airliner laden with fuel, near take-off speed, with a problem. This could end very badly: running off the runway into the sea, an engine fire on a fully loaded plane, who knows. But it was happening, right then and there.

I didn't panic. I simply didn't know what to think. In the moment, I did a complete inventory of my life in what seemed an eternal amount of time. I had no regrets. No relationships unresolved. My wife and my children knew I truly loved them. I always knew my parents loved me, right from an early age. No doubts about that. My extended family always met in joy and respect. My friends would remember the warmth of our interactions. I held no vendettas.

Then I realized my slight tinge of regret was this: *I had not fully shared what I knew with the world*. But even then, plenty of others had also heard what the Three Principles had to offer. In their own ways, they were actively spreading the message of innate wholeness.

The plane came to a stop before the end of the runway. We did not know what had happened. We stayed still in our seats. The airport fire trucks eventually turned up, followed by an aircraft tug. The pilot mentioned something about a technical problem, and that was all. We were towed to the terminal, and we disembarked. We waited in the business class lounge, then caught another plane to our destination and arrived uneventfully.

It turned out the pilot had inadvertently left the brakes on, which explained the slow take-off roll. While the engines were powering us forward, the brakes were holding us back. How apt! A tire had burst under the strain, which was the bang and the lurch we experienced. It was touch and go whether the plane would even stop, given the state of the tires and the brakes. But it did.

And now that I have completed this book, I have no regrets at all.

ACKNOWLEDGMENTS

This book is the culmination of a long journey that started in my childhood. Like most people, I needed to make sense of the world, but found that answers were slow in coming. I am forever indebted to Sydney Banks, who tirelessly communicated his insight into the true nature of the human experience, and provided the missing link between ourselves and the ultimate reality we are a part of.

Syd said that no matter where you are in the world, at the right time, the right person will come and tell you what need to know. As my imaginary journey continued, many people took the time to reach out to me and guide me in the right direction. I am indebted to you all, but several deserve special mention.

First, Judith, my wife of 25 years and counting. When you first get married, you may have an inkling that life will take you in unexpected directions. We had no idea we'd share such a profound spiritual journey together, and that she would find the answer first.

Gilly Chater has been my guide throughout my journey. She introduced me to the Principles and then always pointed me in the right direction when required. Elsie Spittle has been a fantastic teacher and mentor, deepening my understanding of the principles.

Keith Blevens and Valda Monroe provided fresh insights from their own deep spiritual knowledge when I was ready to hear them. They helped me discover which direction *inside* was so I could learn to live from there.

Ricardo Hildago appeared out of the universe to deepen my understanding even more, completing the inquiry on the apparent duality of life that Syd sparked.

As I developed my ideas and sounded them out some very special people went out of their way to give practical advice and emotional support. Avi Liran, of Joy-Care leadership heard my first talk on calm and has continued to provide practical support to give it a proper airing. Mike Matthews, of Twisting Thinking provided that vital corporate view as we tried to make the concepts relevant to the high-pressure workplace. Martha Tara Lee, of Eros Coaching, Singapore's only sexologist, showed me the way to have the courage to get fully behind what you really believe in. Dr Yvonne Looi, the professional joyologist, continued to show by her example that life is, at it's heart, not a serious matter at all.

The practical business of producing a book is both simpler and harder than I imagined. Thank you to Jo-anne Flinn, now known as the artist Booth Aster, another corporate cat who had the courage to do what she was meant to do. Booth mentored me and encouraged me to take the plunge and fully express my ideas. She was also instrumental in my meeting Raymond Aaron, whose practical approach to book writing and branding has been a powerful component of getting this written. Gina Romero, rock-chick entrepreneur and founder of 'Business Rocks' (motto: "it's just like TED, but with beer") has been instrumental in introducing me to a number of fantastic people, most notably Guy Vincent. Guy is founder of Publishizer (www.publishizer.com), a crowd-sourcing, lean-startup, book creation company. As well as enabling a very successful pre-sales campaign, Guy also came up with the title, or rather, cut it down. "Why don't you just call it 'CALM'" he said. Guy introduced me to Sheamus Burns, who created the cover and the layout. You can't judge a book from its cover, but having a great one sure is a great help. Guy also introduced me to the ERIIN girls: Kate Tan and Maisha Miranda, who provided me with that much needed Gen Y perspective and set up a great social media presence. (www.eriin.com).

The Asia Professional Speakers Singapore has been my key "work" organization for the last two years. There is a profound generosity of spirit in the association, and I am indebted to the all the practical advice As I developed my ideas and sounded them out, several people went out provided, freely given. In particular, the Authorship Mastermind group has provided great encouragement and insightful feedback. Lindley Craig (Raise your BAR), Titus Yong and Wendy Tan Siew Lee (Wholeness) have made significant contributions. A number of the true speaking professionals: Certified Speaking Professionals, have freely given a substantial amount their time to help the cause: Fredrik Härén and Rob Salisbury in particular.

Dorothea Brandin (www.ccc.sg) is a gifted coach and helped me over a huge stumbling block: adequately describing the principles. So we sat down one day, and she just listened in her mindful way as I talked them through. The chapter on the principles is a verbatim record of what I said.

One of the things I discovered about writing a good book is that the key is to have a great editor. Barbara McNichol (www.barbaramcnichol.com) has been instrumental in turning a loose collection of ideas into a coherent story. She is a delight to work with and extremely competent in her approach: The right balance of creativity and rigor.

A picture tells a thousand works, but in Tim Hamons case (www.art-of-awakening.com), he has the gift of translating what you said into what you should have said, and presenting it in a new, insightful way. Tim is responsible for the illustrations in the book.

There is a very special mention for a set of people who not only gave their help for free, they made a substantial financial contribution to getting this book completed and finished through the publishizer campaign. These are the founders of the calm revolution:

Bill Jamieson (yes, my Dad!)

Bill and Jackie Goodyear, Australia

Kaye Barnett, New Zealand

Marco Kerkmeester. Santa Grao Café, Brazil

Guy Vincent, Publishizer, Singapore

Gilly Chater, Cordon-Bleu Leadership, New Zealand (www.gillychater.com)

Lindley Craig, All In The Mind, Singapore (www.allinthemind.asia)

Keith MacDonald, Partner, Ernst & Young, UK

David Horne, UK

Amanda McRae, UK

Richard van Laar-Veth, Program Director, Australia/New Zealand

Yasmine Khater, Adventurer, Coach, Speaker, Singapore (www.yasminekhater.com)

Yves-Pascal Pelcener, Leadership and Executive Coach, France/Singapore

In addition, there the hundreds of you who bought the book through Publishizer before it was published. Thank you for your act of faith.

There are many more, of course, and you know who you are. Every time you made contact—a simple gesture, a voice of concern, an arm around a shoulder, a word of simple encouragement—we make a profound connection that means everything. Thank you from the bottom of my heart.

And finally, my two children, Hannah and Ben, who taught me how to love unconditionally. What a beautiful world they will inherit now that we know, with *absolute certainty*, that we are innately whole.

ABOUT THE AUTHOR

After earning a degree in psychology and an MBA, Mark Jamieson embarked on a career in senior management that's taken him across the world and immersed him in multiple cultures. He's devoted time and talent to a number of high-profile corporations, including IBM, Ernst & Young, IBM (again), Oracle, Electronic Data Systems (EDS), and IBM (yet again!).

Drawing on this experience, Mark became aware that something was missing in the way people viewed their working lives and in how they behaved. They were exceedingly busy—but not effectively so. He also detected a notable lack of harmony and success in a multitude of business projects and meetings around him. But why?

In 2001, Mark learned about a model of human experience based on the Three Principles of Mind, Consciousness, and Thought that provided the missing link. This rational model explains how people create their own realities as they interact with the world. Using these Three Principles, he developed an approach for effective and harmonious proceedings and desired results. He calls it CALM.

Today, Mark lives in Singapore and is committed to spreading this understanding to business people who can get things done with insight, not stress.

To find out more, go to:

    http://www.thecalmrevolution.com

    https://www.facebook.com/jointhecalmrevolution

    twittter: @thecalmrev

www.ingramcontent.com/pod-product-compliance
Lightning Source LLC
Chambersburg PA
CBHW050639160426
43194CB00010B/1738